Call Center Rocket Science

110 Tips to Creating a World Class Customer Service Organization

By

Randy Rubingh

CONTENTS

Introduction

I once heard it said running a call center is not rocket science. While it may be true successful call center management does not require the skills and education of an aerospace engineer, call centers do have their own vocabulary and strategies that lead to success. After spending twenty-five years working in call centers, I wanted to put down some of the helpful things I've learned along the way that represent in a very real sense the science—and the art—of running a successful customer service organization. I've tried to be practical and offer real world solutions to real problems, and avoid the "happy talk" that I believe is too prevalent in our industry.

My hope is call center staff with all levels of experience—CSRs, leads, front line supervisors, quality coaches, trainers, managers, directors, and VPs of service—will find ideas in *Call Center Rocket Science* they can use to improve their center and make it a better place for themselves, their agents, and their customers. If you find just one or two ideas and implement them, I hope you consider the book was a worthwhile investment of your time. You'll notice sometimes information is repeated in one or more tips. This is intentional, as the tips are meant to be able to stand alone. This way if you direct someone in your organization to read a certain tip, they have enough information to take action.

It's been said when you steal from one person it's plagiarism, and when you steal from many it's research. A lot of "research" has gone into this book. Many of the ideas and tips in this book are not original. I've always tried to pick out the best ideas I hear from others and incorporate them into the operations of my centers. I have a lot of people to thank for the great ideas I have "stolen" from them. To those people who have helped me along the way and taught me this business, I offer my thanks. This book would not have been possible if not for the many hours spent brainstorming how to improve call centers with JSI, SP, MB, MR, MG, DC, GV, DB, RW, JG, MS, and others too numerous to mention.

I would love to hear your ideas and tips as well. Please visit us at **www.callcenterrocketscience.com** to submit ideas for inclusion in future editions of *Call Center Rocket Science*.

Finally, a big thanks to my family for putting up with the hours and travel of a customer service professional—Kelly, Nicholas, and Christopher, I love you. I could not have done it without you.

Sincerely,

Randy

March, 2013

Section I:
Recruiting and Hiring Tips

Hire well. I believe the single most important thing one can do to improve service in any organization is to hire well. More than anything else, the success of your center hinges on the ability to recruit and hire top talent and good reps. However, with the low prestige of call center work, the strictness of punctuality policies, and the low pay, this can be a very difficult task. This chapter contains ideas on how to recruit and hire the best possible staff for your call center.

Tip 1:
Recruit Better and Save Money by Paying More

At a recent seminar I asked the audience for a show of hands of how many people thought their call center reps were the most important brand ambassadors in their company. All hands went up. I followed up that question with, "How many of you pay them to reflect their status as being that influential to your brand?" Not surprisingly all hands went down as nervous laughter filled the room.

We view the call center as an entry-level position and pay accordingly. Because of the large percentage of company employees in the call center, call center labor costs are a high proportion of the overall company budget and the customer service organization is pressured to keep CSRs salaries low. As a result, it is difficult to find good employees who can deliver high quality service and who are committed to the organization for the long term.

And it's true that if you hire hundreds of agents, paying even one dollar an hour more will add up very quickly. This is of course why call centers traditionally, especially for lower skilled positions, offer low rates of pay- usually about 20% above minimum wage. This low rate of pay does save money in the short run. However, when you began to consider the different levels of agents and add in the total cost per rep per transaction, you will likely find investing in higher qualified reps will save you money in the long run. For example, consider the scenario of hiring reps at $12 per hour vs. $14.40, a 20% premium. If you have one hundred agents, the difference between these salaries is about $500,000 annually, and it may seem prohibitive to consider raising salaries to that level. But let's assume with the higher rate of pay you can hire more skilled reps, resulting in higher first call resolution, and increased productivity and quality scores. As your first call resolution increases, callbacks are reduced. Combined with the higher productivity it is reasonable to assume you now only need eighty-five agents where you previously needed one hundred. The higher skilled agents also mean you can sustain a higher ratio of reps to supervisors, and you will not need to do as much QA monitoring, saving in QA costs.

With the higher rate of agent pay, however, you will also need to raise the rates you pay your supervisors. But let's assume you spend the same total amount, now just divided among six supervisors instead of eight.

Now let's also assume the higher rate of pay reduces attrition, saving you recruiting expenses and the training costs associated with a typical three week new hire training course. As the below table indicates, your costs are now virtually identical.

Reps	Rate Of Pay	Annual Rep Cost	Super- visors Required	Super- visor Cost	Attri- tion Rate	Cost Of Attrition Training	Total Cost (before real estate)
100	$12.00	$2,496,000	8	$288,000	60%	$86,400	$2,870,400
85	$14.40	$2,545,920	6	$288,000	25%	$36,720	$2,870,640

Twenty percent increase in rep pay, identical overall cs costs.

This does not take into account savings in real estate and equipment costs. When these are factored in, those numbers will certainly result in an overall savings from increasing the pay 20%. In addition to this savings, with the higher pay you will find a much more satisfied and engaged staff, resulting in overall higher quality of service offered to your customers.

Tip 2:
Referral Bonuses

Recruiters often cite the best way to find qualified applicants is to seek referrals from current company employees. Employee referrals are usually the least expensive and one of the most effective ways of finding new staff. This is certainly true in the call center. Representatives in your call center usually know people who are looking for work or people who may be interested in changing jobs. Because they know the job so well, and presumably they know their friends well, they'll know if the person is going to be a good fit in customer service. As a result, employee referrals have a much higher chance of success than candidates sourced and interviewed by even the most savvy and discerning recruiters.

In addition, you can trust your employees will be honest with their friends about what they like and dislike about working in your center. This allows referral candidates to have a clear idea of what they're getting themselves into, and they can make a well-informed decision about whether they really want to come to work in the demanding call center environment.

Monetary bonuses are a great way to encourage employee referrals. While some suggest monetary bonuses might lead employees to refer anyone in hopes of a payout, the truth is most employees will not risk their reputation by referring someone they don't think will be successful. The bonus really serves as a reminder and an encourager to solicit referrals.

Bonuses should be contingent upon the new employee graduating from training and satisfactorily completing a probationary period. This ensures there are no payouts if either the organization or the employee decides this is not a good fit.

The amount for a referral bonus should be dependent on the difficulty in hiring for the position. The bonus needs to be high enough to motivate reps to encourage their friends and colleagues to apply for positions. The equivalent of two weeks' salary is an amount reps often find motivating, and is a great deal for you in terms of recruiting costs.

Tip 3:
Always Be Recruiting

A good recruiter is always recruiting. Encourage your recruiters and management staff to always carry around business cards and give them out to friendly people they meet who may be potential candidates for current, or future call center positions. You should do the same.

For example, if you encounter a person with a friendly personality at your local coffee shop or when buying a pair of shoes, hand them one of your business cards and say, "I run a call center and you seem like someone who would be a great call center rep. If either you or someone you know is interested at some point in the future, give me a call." Because retail jobs and coffee shops have high turnover, friendly people in these positions are not only great candidates, but are often available – and you've already seen the positive attitude they display at their work. The continual recruiting of people you meet in service positions will help build the pipeline of available candidates.

In addition, you should always have an open position listed on your website. Even if you're not currently hiring, this helps build an applicant pool. Then when you do start a hiring cycle you will, hopefully, have a pool of recent applicants. Having to suddenly recruit twenty or thirty reps is an extremely difficult task if you're starting without an existing base or pipeline.

Tip 4:
Teach a Community Center Class

One way to meet a pool of potential applicants is to have some-one from either your training or recruiting team teach a computer or similar entry level skill class at a local community center. While providing a valuable job skill to people in the local community, you'll encounter many potential applicants, some of whom may be taking the class with the goal of learning skills to find a job similar to the one you have to offer. This may give you first crack at qualified applicants soon to hit the job market. And as their teacher, you'll have had enough opportunity to interact with them to know their communication skills, as well as to observe their attendance and punctuality habits. At the end of the course, in addition to performing a community service, you may find you have a substantial number of the applicants you need for your next class.

Tip 5:
Build a Recruiting Story

Many customer service organizations have rules stating an employee cannot transfer to another department until they have served in their original department for a set amount of time, usually ranging from six to eighteen months. While it's understandable customer service departments want to recoup training costs, this can be shortsighted. Using customer service as a training ground for positions in the rest of the company is actually very good for the call center and its management team.

First, the career progression of staff moving from the call center to other departments builds a compelling recruiting story. It's very powerful to tell new recruits specific success stories of employees in other departments who started their company career in the call center. Such a story may provide a highly qualified recruit the incentive and motivation to take a call center position as a stepping-stone to achieving their ultimate career goals. While this individual may spend less time as a CSR than you would like, having a revolving door of highly qualified agents will benefit you more than average performing employees who stay longer.

In addition to the recruiting benefit, talented people placed throughout the company are a valuable source of contacts. If you have helped CSRs to transfer to other departments, chances are if you need something from another department you can find a call center alumnus to help you.

Former reps working in other departments also help foster a more customer-centric approach to the organization. They have seen firsthand how a "small" issue that may seem like it will have negligible customer impact, often will result in calls from frustrated or confused customers.

Tip 6:
Look for Motivated Candidates

You'll encounter many applicants who are willing to work in your center. However for a portion of your applicants a CSR position is not their first choice; it's simply their only current option to avoid being unemployed. Hiring a rep with such an attitude may eventually lead to problems. Do everything you can to ascertain if the applicant considers a call center position to be a good, long-term position, or at least a good stepping-stone in their career progression. For many applicants this may be their first office job, and therefore a position they consider worthy of respect and dedication. Others, especially those coming from a retail environment, will like the consistency of hours, as well as not having to be on their feet all day and not having to work with customers face to face. Such reps will be far more appreciative of their position, even if they consider it entry level.

On the other hand, if the rep considers the job beneath them, at best they will only work a short amount of time before seeking other employment, and at worst they will infect other staff with their poor attitude. To understand if a call center position is something that will be a good fit for them, thoroughly explore the candidate's background and especially probe their attitude. Only hire those who believe the job is a worthwhile profession.

Tip 7:
Pros and Cons of Using an Employment Agency

It's not easy to hire the right people. In the call center we hire a lot of people, and the majority of them do not bring much work experience. Even the most perceptive interviewer and hiring manager will make mistakes, especially as they will often be under pressure to hire quickly to fill a scheduled and impending training class. By leveraging the service of an employment agency (often referred to as a temp agency), you can easily remedy hiring miscalculations. If there's a case of a bad hire, or you simply find the new employee is not a good fit, or you no longer need the rep, this can be resolved with a simple call to the agency you work with. They will notify the employee their assignment is over, saving you the time, paperwork, hassle, and stress associated with terminating the employment of one of your company's full time, regular employees. You'll pay a premium to the agency until you decide to either let the employee go or convert them to permanent status (usually ninety days). But if you hire large numbers of call center reps and end up having to let a fair amount go, this strategy can save you a lot of management time and money in the long run.

Note however, I'm not advocating using a temp or employment agency to exclusively source candidates. I recommend you interview and screen applicants yourself. Once you find an employee you would like to hire, have them enroll with the agency and then hire them through the agency for a ninety-day trial or probationary period. At that point if you want to retain them, convert them to a permanent status. There is some minor risk that during the probationary period a good employee might leave for a permanent job at another company, but this is often outweighed by the time you'll save in having to deal with a bad hire.

Even with the above advantages, using temps is not the best strategy for all centers. Under normal circumstances someone who is already employed will not leave their permanent position for a temporary position at your company. As a result your ability to recruit top talent may be limited, as you're mostly drawing from a pool of those currently unemployed. In addition, having a mix of contract and permanent employees can set up an environment of "haves and have nots." This can create negative effects on your culture.

Before you determine if you want to hire direct or through an agency, consider the pros and cons, as well as the employment laws in your state. Generally speaking, if the rate of pay you offer is at the high end compared to similar jobs in your local talent pool, hiring direct is the more effective strategy as you're able to attract strong, experienced candidates, and have lower risk of hiring mistakes. But if you offer rates of pay low compared to similar companies, it's likely you won't be able to attract the top candidates. Plus, if you find more of the reps you are hiring are currently unemployed, you're likely to have more issues. If that's the situation you find yourself in, the agency route is to your advantage.

Tip 8:
Multiple Touch Point Hiring Process

To succeed in the call center agents need to be extremely reliable, show up every day, and show up on time. A best practice to determine if a candidate can meet the strict punctuality requirements of the call center is to establish a system where candidates have to keep multiple appointments during the application process. In addition to giving you a preview of the candidate's punctuality and attendance habits, the multiple touch point hiring process will weed out many applicants who really aren't interested in working in your center. They just need a job, and any job will do.

Here's an example of a five-touch-point hiring process:

Touch point 1: The applicant comes in at a set time to fill out an application. This appointment is set after they first express interest in response to your advertisement or through an employee referral. Do not allow candidates to simply come in and fill out an application at their leisure. If they walk in and ask to apply, do not let someone hand them an application. Schedule an appointment. Filling out the application is your first touch point to see if they can make it on time. While they're in the office for this first test touch point, ask them to fill out the application using a computer. To get a rough idea of how comfortable they are with the computer, casually watch them. Usually this means just observing if they are very *uncomfortable* with the computer. If so, they will likely have a difficult time succeeding in your call center.

Also, observe how prepared they came. Were they able to fill out job history and reference information, particularly if you told them to bring this information to the appointment?

Randy Rubingh

Touch point 2: Arrange and schedule a phone interview. Again, do not simply call and began talking with the applicant, rather set up a phone interview appointment for a predetermined time.

Touch point 3: Next, ask the applicant to come in for an initial screen and interview, usually conducted by a member of your recruiting or human resources department. During this touch point the applicant should be given some sort of prescreening test. This can be as simple as a basic typing test, or a basic grammar and vocabulary test. Depending on the position and the level of experience required, it may be appropriate for the assessment to include some technical skills questions as well.

Touch point 4: Have another round of interviewing with the hiring manager and members of the customer service team.

Touch point 5: Ask the applicant to come in for an offer letter and acceptance meeting.

While it would certainly be faster and more convenient to schedule some of these all at once or to give the offer over the phone, having so many touch points helps you screen out applicants who may have transportation issues, struggle with punctuality beyond an initial interview, or those who are simply not dedicated. Do not view these touch points as bureaucratic or excessive. The more touch points you have the more effectively you will weed out future problems.

Tip 9:
Allow Applicants to Listen to Calls

Another effective way to allow potential reps to weed themselves out during the application process is to have applicants listen to calls during their initial on-site interview. For fifteen minutes before you begin the discussion portion of the interview have the applicant listen to calls, either side-by-side with a senior rep or remotely. Then you can ask them about what they heard. You can see how attentive they were and get a sense of their listening skills. By asking how they would feel taking these types of calls you can also gauge their reaction to having to answer call after call, day after day. Remember this job isn't for everyone. Many applicants who have listened to calls will decide not to go further in the interview process. If you have a multiple touch point process in place they simply won't follow through with the next step, saving the applicant from accepting a job that is not a good fit, and saving you a potential hiring mistake.

Tip 10:
Utilize Reps as Part of the Interview Team

A complete interviewing team can offer more robust feedback on candidates than a single individual. To round out your interview team include at least one customer service rep. The role of the CSR is to help the candidates understand what the job is like, both good and bad. Further, reps are usually very effective at recognizing qualities that will make a successful peer. Interviewing someone can also be considered a mark of career progression for representatives. Before allowing reps to interview though, be sure to train them on interviewing techniques and the legal aspects of interviewing. Make sure they are aware what can and cannot be asked. It's a good practice to invite a rep to observe an interview or two before actively participating in the process.

Tip 11:
Do a Quick Test for Email and Chat Reps

For many centers phone calls are now a minority of the customer interactions. The representatives you hire may be expected to take chat and email contacts in addition to phone calls. If this is true in your center, interview candidates using the channels they will be supporting

If they'll be answering email or chat, set them up in an interview room and email or chat with them from another room. This doesn't have to be an extensive part of the interview process. Simply having the candidate respond to a couple questions through email or chat will give you a clear idea of how well the candidate communicates using these channels. Remember, writing is a completely different skill set than talking on the phone. Most managers wouldn't put someone on the phone to whom they haven't talked, so why do we place reps on chat or email when we have no indication of how they communicate using these media? Taking a few minutes to do this during the interview process can greatly increase the quality of reps you hire. This is especially critical if you are hiring reps who will do solely email or chat support.

Tip 12:
The Interview Agenda

While the interview does involve several steps and components, it doesn't need to take up too much of your time. See the sample agenda below, and note, as a manager you're only investing fifteen minutes for each candidate. And while sixty-five minutes total may seem like a lot if you're hiring many CSRs, this agenda will give you and your team a clear picture of the person you're interviewing, while at the same time providing the candidate an equally clear picture of what the job entails. The time spent will allow many candidates for whom the position is not a good match to realize this up front and take themselves out of the running as candidates.

Sample Interview Agenda:

1. Greet applicant and provide them with an agenda (5 minutes).
2. Applicant listens to calls, side by side or remote (15 minutes).
3. Have them talk with the team, including CSRs (20 minutes).
4. Have them answer a couple questions through chat or email (10 minutes).
5. Wrap up with hiring manager interview (15 minutes).

Tip 13:
The Actual Interview

When you interview potential customer service reps, there are a couple things you're trying to determine and skills you want to assess. What is this person's ability to effectively communicate our products and services? What is their potential as a CSR?

The successful rep will need to possess a combination of both technical and customer service skills. To determine a candidate's technical expertise you may have a written test, a series of questions you ask them, or you may even bring in technical experts to quiz the candidate. Most CSR positions however, are not so technical they require previous, specialized training. For more general customer service positions you only need to understand the candidate's ability to learn and communicate effectively. Here are some suggestions to help you determine if you're looking at the right person for your position.

1) Start by asking candidates about their experience with social networking or other internet sites. Really all you want to understand is whether they're staying up on current technical and social trends. Having a social media account certainly is not a qualifier or disqualifier for the position, but it does infer the candidate is familiar with online etiquette and resources. This is especially important for CSRs who provide email or chat support. And all call center positions require some computer and online skills, so having a social network account usually means the candidate at least knows how to navigate a computer and the internet.

2) See if they can educate you on something you're unfamiliar with. Ask the candidate to describe technical aspects from a previous position. You're looking to see if they're able to

start with very general and easy-to-understand language, and move on to more technical concepts easily.

3) Throw in a couple of trickier questions. For example, ask candidates to describe a poor customer service experience they have recently experienced. Then ask them how they would have handled the same situation if they had been the customer service representative in that position and were required to stick to the policy. Somewhat surprisingly this often is a difficult question for candidates, and tends to reveal their attitude in difficult situations. Do not be concerned with the answer as much as to how quickly and easily the applicant is able to navigate the question.

4) Punctuality and attendance are extremely important in a service environment. Of course, all but the most clueless candidates will claim to be extremely reliable and punctual. So instead of asking the question directly, start by talking about your company culture and how you like to be sure to treat all employees fairly. Then ask what experiences they have had with companies with unfair policies. I have been amazed over the years with the number of interviewees who described "unfair" punctuality and attendance policies. Policies very similar to the same ones they would be under if they became a CSR in my organization.

Tip 14:
Look for Laughter During the Interview

A good indication of a future successful CSR is whether they laugh quickly and easily. A quick laugh reveals a friendly personality and the enthusiastic tone you're looking for. While it's true some CSR positions require a serious tone, almost all positions benefit from friendly people. I'm not saying you're looking for people who make jokes on the phone. But I am saying someone who laughs easily demonstrates friendliness and the ability to connect with other people, which are two important qualities for someone in customer service. I usually start interviews casually and look for ways to inject humor to see how the person responds. In addition to "testing" for friendliness, it also helps relax the candidate and can help me get a clearer picture of how they will respond to work in a call center.

Tip 15:
Close Good Candidates With a Tour

You'll typically conduct many interviews before finding a good candidate. When you do find a good one you want to do everything you can to create a positive impression of your department, and motivate the candidate to join your team. Remember, better candidates will have more options when choosing a job. A simple and effective way of selling your company to a candidate you want to hire is to give them a brief tour of your center and introduce them to key staff members you encounter. The tour and introductions are a great personal touch, and will leave a positive impression on candidates who are faced with a choice of employment opportunities.

Tip 16:
Write Down Your Feedback

After an interview it's important to immediately write down feedback regarding candidates. Typically you'll talk to many candidates, and it will be difficult to recall which ones your preferred and why. Include in your notes a score for each question, not only for what each candidate said, but how they said it, and the attitude they displayed throughout the interview. Form your decisions using all three criteria. Keep in mind most employees will do as you train them, so the specific answers to questions are not as important as the candidate's mental agility and attitude. If you note observations and score each of these areas you'll more easily be able to sort through the dozens of candidates later, even as they start to become a blur.

Tip 17:
Customer Service vs. Technical Skills

Sometimes when choosing a new customer service rep you have to choose between one candidate who appears to be more qualified technically but does not seem to have good customer service skills, and another candidate who is not as technically strong but who appears to possess superior customer service skills. Generally speaking unless you're recruiting for a very technical position, it's better to choose the candidate with the better customer service skills. While it might take time to train the applicant on the technical skills you require, you're more likely to be successful training on technical skills than you are to train someone to be great with customers.

Similar to the baseball adage "you can't train speed," in the call center "you can't train friendliness." Sure, you can train most people to recite a proper greeting and a proper closing, but tone is one of the more difficult things to train. It's much easier to train someone on technical skills than to answer the phone with the needed enthusiasm. Ask yourself, "Where will this person be in sixty days in terms of their skill levels?" In sixty days most agents will have the required technical expertise regardless of where they started, but if they started with poor communication or customer skills, they will likely still be struggling in these areas.

Tip 18:
Pros and Cons of Call Center Experience

It's natural, and important, to look for experience when evaluating candidates for any position. When assessing candidates for call center positions, however, don't place too much emphasis on prior experience. Remember, the call center is a job with a high burnout rate. If someone is burned out they often think a change in environment will help. And it usually does, but only temporarily. Hiring a rep already burned out will get you an experienced, burned-out rep. Burnout can be contagious and bad attitudes spread quickly.

Also, because of high turnover, most call centers advance good reps into higher positions fairly quickly. While this is not always the case, it's certainly something to be explored. If an applicant has been working as a front line rep for more than three years, you'll want to probe carefully to see if there is a reason they have not progressed to a higher position. It might simply be the call centers they have worked do not offer many opportunities for advancement. But if they worked in a mid-size to large center and have not advanced, chances are there is a reason for it beyond lack of opportunity. You want to ensure you're not getting a burned-out rep who hasn't proven worthy of promotion at their current or former employer.

Tip 19:
Create a Balanced Staff

An important factor to consider when selecting candidates is how the individual balances your team. Of course you're always looking to select the most qualified candidate, but part of someone's qualifications is how well their skills mesh with the rest of your team. For example, if you have CSRs with great interpersonal and customer service skills, but who aren't strong in technical areas, you may want to continue your search until you find someone with a really strong technical background for your next hire.

Having a mix of ages and backgrounds makes for a well-rounded team, and helps staff better relate to customers who are in a different demographic than themselves. You'll also want a mix of individuals with flexible schedules to ensure you don't have coverage issues down the road. You never want to hire weaker candidates, but simply focus on creating a balanced team. Take into account the needs of the team and how candidates complement the existing team's strengths and weaknesses when deciding who to hire next, especially in small centers.

Tip 20:
Be Patient When Hiring

While this may seem obvious, this tip is difficult to follow when under pressure. When requisitions don't get approved until you're under the gun, service levels have already deteriorated, and you have a training session starting in two days and five open slots remain, you'll try to talk yourself into hiring mediocre applicants.

Don't do it. If you're really desperate, look for other resources to help you during the crisis or hire candidates through a temp agency. Even if you sourced them yourself, you can still have them sign up through an agency. This will cost you a premium, but this insurance is certainly worth it. Rarely does a mediocre candidate turn into a good rep, let alone a great one. It's true you can fill your training class by compromising your standards a little, but think about the hours you will need to spend documenting, coaching, and eventually dismissing a mediocre representative. Be confident your customers would rather hold a minute longer and talk with a good rep, than be answered right away by someone who is unable or unwilling to help them.

Tip 21:
The Elusive Soccer Mom

Whenever I talk to an outsourcing service company about their pool of candidates, they inevitably bring up part-time employees who like to work while the kids are in school—otherwise known as soccer moms. My personal experience is soccer moms are the Sasquatch of the call center industry. You hear about them but they are rarely, if ever, encountered. However, just because they are more rare than rumored or promised does not mean they don't exist. So if you find an educated soccer mom who would like to work in your call center, I would generally advise you be willing to make concession regarding schedules and flexibility to hire her, even if such concessions are not normally allowed in your center. The trade-off you make for allowing an educated, experienced representative to determine their own schedule will easily be made up in quality and satisfaction of your customers.

Tip 22:
Post-Training Feedback Session

A fter the conclusion of training, coordinate a meeting between the training and recruiting teams. The purpose of this meeting is for the trainers to give feedback to the recruiters on how success-ful the hiring process was based on the time training has spent with the recent hires. Use these feedback sessions to refine and improve the hiring process. During this meeting review:

- Who performed well during training? Was the recruiting team able to predict which individuals would stand out? Can we use their prior experience or responses during the inter-view to update our candidate profile?

- Who struggled in the class? Why did we decide to hire them? Were there any red flags during the hiring process that we didn't pay close enough attention to?

- Who dropped out of the class? What were the earliest signs this person was not going to be successful? Was there a way to determine this before an offer was made?

This post-training meeting strengthens the front end of the interview process and provides critical feedback to the hiring team. Over time you'll find this greatly improves and fine-tunes the interview pro-cess.

Section II
Training Tips

Other than hiring the right people, the single most important factor influencing your customer's experience is the training of your agents. Training is the foundation of your service center. You can do a lot of things to build a great service center, but if the foundation is weak the business will never reach its full potential. With a firm foundation you can layer one building block after another to create a successful and strong enterprise.

Training, especially new hire training, not only provides the baseline of information your customer service reps need when interacting with your customers, but also sets the tone and establishes the culture of your center. A rep's first few days of employment are critical in understanding the way you do things. If the company training is disorganized and without clear goals, your employees will assume their work can also be disorganized and without clear goals. But if the training that you provide is positive, enriching, encouraging, well organized, and respectful, your reps will more likely emulate these attributes and treat your customers with the same values.

Tips 23-39 focus on the new hire experience and creating a great new hire training program. The remaining training tips are more general in nature, relating to ongoing training or specific items to train to.

Tip 23:
Hire a Professional Trainer

Many call centers, especially those with less than fifty seats, appoint a subject matter expert as the department trainer. This makes logical sense and, on the surface, seems like a good idea.

However, being a subject matter expert hardly qualifies someone to impart expertise to someone else. Even if a professional trainer is not the most knowledgeable person on a particular subject they're probably the right person to administer the training. Students under them will leave class with a better grasp of the material than they would from a subject matter expert who is not well versed in training techniques.

Consider this: On a scale of 0 to 100, if a trainer has a knowledge level of 70 and can get reps to understand and retain 80% of what he or she teaches, reps will leave the training class with the knowledge level of 56. A subject matter expert may have a knowledge level of 90, but if he only imparts 50% of that knowledge, reps leave the class with a knowledge level of only 45.

Subject matter expert:

Knowledge level 90 x 50% imparted = 45 knowledge level.

Professional Trainer:

Knowledge level 70 x 80% imparted = 56 knowledge level.

In addition, new call center reps generally only learn a baseline of information during their initial training. Typically they learn the more complicated details of the position over time, or in future training sessions after they've gained experience. Therefore, it's not important to have the person who can go into the most granular details train your new hires. Rather, it's important the training be done by the person who can best impart the knowledge required by new hires for their first days on the floor.

If you choose a trainer from your existing staff, do so carefully. Look for someone who's organized, has good presentation skills, and can generate enthusiasm for your products and services. On more advanced topics, particularly with ongoing training, it may be beneficial or even necessary to have a subject matter expert alongside the trainer to answer questions or fill in the blanks. But even in these situations it's more effective to have your trainer train, and the subject matter expert available to interject at key points or take questions, not teach the entire class. An exception to this would be when the training is part of a personal development opportunity for a subject matter expert who desires to eventually become a trainer, or at least develop skills in this area.

If you do hire an experienced, professional trainer, they will bring an understanding of adult learning methods that will greatly enhance the experience of your new employees. Experienced trainers keep trainees engaged *and* maximize learning. They have been taught to understand the three fundamental learning styles—auditory, visual, and kinesthetic—and how to adapt lessons so all three types of learners are engaged.

In addition, a professional trainer will provide documentation and learning materials. Creating good documentation is critical to achieving consistency and continuity in your training program and center as a whole. When you don't have training classes running, the full-time trainer becomes a valuable resource for ongoing training, as well as documenting policies and procedures.

If the budget to hire a professional trainer is an issue, look to hire a less experienced trainer who would be willing to assume supervisor, quality monitor, or even part-time rep responsibilities. You'll still enjoy the benefits of having a professional trainer on staff, and have an additional part-time resource. If you do this however, keep in mind developing a good training curriculum and class agenda requires extensive prep time. In order to maximize the effectiveness of your part-time trainer, you'll need to allow them time to adequately prepare for the classes. A general rule of thumb is it takes eight hours of preparation for every hour of instruction in the classroom.

Tip 24:
Train During Shift Hours

Typically training is conducted during standard business hours. But if you're hiring customer service reps to work a night shift it's best to train during the night. If you're hiring for swing shift, best to train during the swing shift. It may be inconvenient to conduct training during reps eventual shift hours, but this best practice has two advantages:

1) It respects the schedules of the people you hire. A new hire may have selected the late shift because it provides the flexibility to be home during the day when their presence is required for other responsibilities, such as childcare. If you train during the day you're asking them to put those responsibilities on hold for the duration of the training class. While they might be willing to do so, and you should certainly appreciate their flexibility, they may be distracted and unable to fully concentrate.

2) It allows you to observe and correct punctuality issues before reps are on the floor. Transportation may be readily available and punctuality not a concern for someone arriving at 9:00 a.m. for training. However, by starting training at their shift start time of 10:00 p.m., any issues preventing them from arriving on time on a consistent basis will surface. You now have the opportunity to correct this before they hit the floor and it becomes critical that they adhere to scheduled start times.

Of course, this is not always possible to arrange. You may not have enough coverage on some shifts to allow for side-by-side listening or other important activities. Further, you may be hiring people with different shifts and need them to attend the same training class. But to the extent it's possible train your new employees during the shift they will eventually be working.

Tip 25:
Start with Communication Skills

M ost new hire training sessions last two to six weeks, with the first portion centered on the company—its history, purpose, vision, etc. After that, systems are covered. Then the focus shifts to products and services, where the majority of training time is spent. Finally the new hire training concludes with a day of discussion and training of customer communication skills and quality scoring.

This is a logical approach, but reversing the agenda to start with communication skills has the following advantages.

1) It sets the right tone for your center. New reps understand right away you're focused and concerned about customer communication and do not take "soft skills" as an afterthought.

2) You have a framework for all role-playing and examples you'll use during the course. Every time a role-play or example is offered it can be practiced using proper and expected communication techniques. This reinforces those techniques so by the time reps reach the floor they will be comfortable and sound natural.

Compare the following two-week training outlines:

Typical Customer Service Training Outline

Day 1: Company History, Vision, Mission, Values

Day 2: Systems, Introduce Products and Services

Days 3-8: Products and Services

Days 9: Communication Skills

Day 10: Testing and Graduation

Improved Customer Service Training Outline

Day 1: Company History, Vision, Mission, Values

Day 2: Communication Skills

Day 3: Systems, Introduce Products and Services

Days 4-9: Products and Services

Day 10: Testing and Graduation

Inserting communication skills earlier in the agenda provides students a base for role plays and shows its importance.

Tip 26:
Split the Training Class

Depending on the complexity of the material and type of support the reps will be providing, contact center new hire training classes typically run two to six consecutive weeks. A more effective practice though is to split the training class into sections, and give reps floor time in between. For example, instead of being in the classroom for two straight weeks and then graduating to the floor, spend one week in the classroom, then spend the next week on the floor taking simple calls. After that go back into the classroom for the final week of instruction.

You will find this approach has a number of advantages. First, customer service reps who realize they will soon be on the floor will stay on their toes during the initial week of training. They understand there is no time to drift off or catch up later. Getting on the phones is right around the corner.

Most importantly, after a week on the phones your final week of training will become more effective. Trainees will be more attentive during their final week if you split your training this way. In training classes running straight through without interruption reps are often bored by the second week and have trouble paying attention, which is critical as you move into more advanced topics toward the end of training. However if reps have been on the floor for a week, your trainer will find his or her students to be much more attentive. The students realize the challenges they will soon face and will want to take advantage of the training time.

Also, inquisitive trainees often ask questions that may seem important only to someone who's never been on the floor, distracting the trainer from his or her agenda. Once a rep has been on the floor however, the questions will be much more practical, focused, and grounded in the real-world experience of your call center. The trainer will find less need to go into details on concepts that rarely, if ever, come up on the phones.

Finally, the time spent on the phone will solidify the basic concepts learned in the first week of training, making the final week more effective. It's one thing to learn in a classroom and another to be able to apply that information in a real life situation. The in-between week on the phone allows your new hires to solidify the basic information from the first week, get a real understanding of the initial material, and orientate themselves for the final phase of their training.

Tip 27:
Effective Role-Playing

Role-playing and simulating calls is one of the most important aspects of any call center training class. The first time someone answers a question using information recently learned, the answer will inevitably come out awkward and stilted sounding. However, after they have answered the same question aloud ten or more times, a new rep will find answers often roll off their tongue and they sound confident and articulate. Your goal as a call center trainer is to provide a safe classroom environment for the nine awkward attempts, so by the time the agent is talking with real customers the rep sounds like a knowledgeable and experienced agent. The key to doing this is role-playing, role-playing, role-playing....and more role-playing.

A key to effective role-playing is not to allow digression and sidebars. Role-players often break from character to ask questions and seek clarification. This breaks the rhythm of the role-play, which might not get back on track, meaning your rep never has the opportunity to fully answer the question in the training environment. I have audited many training programs and watched hours of role-play sessions without ever seeing a completed call from start to finish, thus losing much of the value of this effective training tool. But when you role-play in a simulated environment where reps proceed as they would with a real customer on the phone, including how to proceed when questions are asked they do not know how to answer, reps grow stronger and more confident. It's much more effective. If needed, they can ask the person role-playing the caller if they can be placed on hold, find the information they need, and return to the call.

The most important aspect of effective role-playing is the use of real-life questions. Too often role-plays consist of the instructor asking theoretical questions and receiving theoretical answers. Or the trainer asking very simple questions, which the trainees can answer but will rarely experience on the phones. This may be fine for beginning the program, but as the students gain experience the questions need to become more practical, which doesn't necessarily mean more difficult. Tricky, difficult questions are not nearly as valuable to the student as practical, real-life questions they will need to answer routinely.

A good way to incorporate real-life questions into role plays is to use recorded calls. Play a recorded call to the training class and after the initial question is asked by the caller, stop the recording and let a rep take over as the agent, and have the instructor assume the role of the caller. When the role play is completed, play the rest of the call to compare the new hire's answer with that of the experienced rep who originally answered the call.

You can also find real-life questions by using emails you have received. Use these questions verbatim to give students practice with actual questions they will soon receive on the phones. Again, you'll find this is much more effective than using made-up questions.

Role-playing can also be a fun group training activity and can build camaraderie amongst your students. One way to do this is first write a script to a question on a whiteboard. Then go around the room in rapid succession and have everyone answer the question. Next cover the whiteboard and go in rapid succession around the room again. Depending on the length of the script it might be appropriate to just erase part of the script, and continue to erase parts until the entire script is erased, and all students can answer the question without the aid of the script.

Another fun option is to have all the students stand up and randomly run through a script in rapid fire. If a student is called upon and they answer using the script correctly they sit down. However, if anyone fails to use the script clearly and completely, everyone has to stand back up and the process begins again. The exercise does not end until everyone is sitting down. Usually this results in reps cheering for each other and building a team spirit.

In the above exercises the role-play serves not only a learning activity, but also fun and helps foster team spirit among classmates. If your classes are becoming dull, try one of these options to inject some life and energy into the class.

As students gain experience, role-plays should evolve into simulations. Simulations incorporate using the computer to access information, enter customer data to track and log calls, and other functions the trainees will eventual soon be required to do in their new positions. Don't consider training complete until trainees have demonstrated the ability to completely answer and simulate calls multiple times.

Tip 28:
Fast Track Training with the Top Ten

In order to qualify and graduate onto the floor, all students should be required to smoothly and correctly answer the top ten questions asked in your center. If they can do this, chances are they'll be an effective rep their first day on the floor. Training classes should develop a curriculum that revolves around the Top Ten.

The idea of knowing the Top Ten is so powerful I have occasionally used a "Fast Track Top Ten" approach to significantly shorten new hire training classes. I've done this when I have found myself in a critical staffing shortage and needed the students on the phone as absolutely soon as possible.

The Top Ten fast track method is to provide students a list of the top ten questions they'll receive from callers, as well as the answer to each question. Then role-play every single question and every single answer. After each student has role-played every question and answer ten times, move on to the computer and begin simulations. After they're able to simulate every call ten times successfully without error, put them on the phones. Again, I would prefer to have students role play and practice the Top Ten within the normal context of an extended training program. But if you find yourself in an emergency situation, simply drilling and having agents become well-versed and practiced at the Top Ten, which usually represents 80% plus of the calls they receive, is likely to be a very effective training despite the abbreviated agenda.

When doing this be sure one of the Top Ten scripts is how to handle a question the rep is unfamiliar with, so trainees can practice proper hold, transfer, or call back techniques for the inevitable calls they receive they will not be able to answer.

Tip 29:
Introduce Other Departments

A constant challenge in every contact center is staying connected to the rest of the company. Too often the call center feels like its own isolated entity. But connecting the service center to the rest of the organization has many benefits. For one, introducing reps to the rest of the company exposes them to opportunities and positions they may one day have the opportunity to apply for. Having a specific career goal to transfer to another department keeps staff motivated and encourages them to do their best. In addition, contacts made with employees in other departments often lead to informal exchanges resulting in improvements to internal systems, the company website, and company products. The value in keeping customer service reps connected to the rest that company can hardly be overestimated.

This connection cannot be made too early. Have other departments become a part of training by having them present their goals, missions, and objectives to your new customer service reps. Ask managers or department heads to spend thirty minutes presenting this information during your new hire training. This helps reps connect the service center with the wider organization. It also helps them identify key players in the company, and understand who to go to for certain types of information.

In addition to other departments, ask the CEO or other senior members of the executive team to come in and speak to the trainees. This helps cement the impression the company is committed to customer service and creates a culture of high standards within service.

Personal contact also allows key managers to see and appreciate the level of talent in customer service. Too often other departments will hear negative feedback regarding service, which will lead to unflattering assumptions regarding the quality and educational level of customer service reps. But once they've met them, these assumptions are often replaced with more positive impressions.

Presentations by other departments also provide a break during training, allowing a trainer to assess how the training is going and make agenda adjustments. Finally, such presentations create a more professional training experience and demonstrate a commitment to service by the rest of the organization.

A word based on experience: it's not always easy to get other departments to come in and present to your training class. While most department heads agree it's a good idea, they're busy and consider such a presentation a luxury rather than a necessity. If you find resistance, don't give up. While it can be challenging for other managers to make time for this on their schedule, once they do they will have a more favorable impression of customer service, and the process helps create a more customer-centric culture within their departments. It's worth championing this initiative.

Presentations by other departments are also a great agenda item for ongoing training. When it's done as part of an ongoing training program there tends to be even more give-and-take, as experienced reps can relate customer issues and feedback to the other departments. This often results in process and technological improvements. In addition, once other departments are exposed to customer service they often see ways they can help service, and become more sensitive to the needs of customers.

Tip 30:
Trainer to Supervisor Hand-Off

I recently met with a group of trainers, and one proudly told me that ninety-five percent of the students in his training class reached graduation. While I certainly did not want to dampen the younger trainer's enthusiasm, I wondered aloud how their hiring process could have been so successful. When hiring in the large numbers, and under the time pressures of the call center environment, it's inevitable some hiring mistakes will be made. Not everyone who starts a training class is right for the position, and the sooner this is discovered and dealt with, the better it's for both the organization and the student. It should be the responsibility of the training department to determine when hiring mistakes have been made, and work with appropriate management to decide next course of action.

A new rep should not graduate from training until a supervisor accepts them onto the floor. If there are any concerns about the representative, the supervisor should have the option to not accept them onto his or her team. When that happens, the training manager can work with the appropriate management members to determine if additional training is required, or if it would be better to end the trainee's employment. On the other hand, once a representative is accepted onto the floor, any performance issues become the responsibility of their new supervisor.

This handoff approach prevents supervisors from having to accept potentially poor performers. As a result, potential performance issues are more likely to be dealt with during the training or probationary period, a time when it's much easier to dismiss an employee who should not have been hired in the first place.

I'm not suggesting the primary role of training is weeding out employees. It's crucial the culture of the training program is one that allows for risk taking. If your reps think that if they make a mistake they'll be fired, the training will be compromised and not nearly as effective. Nevertheless, this is the most appropriate time to deal with issues, especially if reps are hired on a probationary status.

As a follow up, whenever a dismissal from training takes place there should be a debrief between training and those responsible for hiring to see if there was anything during the interview process that might have indicated there was a potential problem. The hiring team needs to use this information to adjust their hiring profiles and interview techniques.

Tip 31:
Assign a Buddy or Mentor

One of the fastest ways to acclimate new reps to your center and culture is to assign them a buddy or mentor on their first day. Ideally this is the rep who will eventually assist them with side-by-side training, but it may just be someone who is very friendly and can help the new employee feel at home in their new work environment. The best "buddies" I have known were not necessarily good at explaining technical aspects of the position, but they were good at making sure new employees had someone to eat lunch with on their first day, informed their new teammates about local lunch spots, and greeted them warmly when they passed in the hallways. These simple gestures go a long way to any new employee. But this is especially true in the highly stressful environment of the service center, where the new employee not only has a challenging job to learn, but also is part of a large department where everyone works in close quarters, and reps see statistics and other performance measures of their peers. Having a buddy can be the difference between feeling overwhelmed and successfully assimilating into a new environment.

A buddy program also helps the experienced rep serving as the mentor. When a rep becomes a buddy it gives him or her the opportunity to demonstrate leadership skills and take on additional responsibility. This is probably a role reps with supervisor ambitions will seek out, thereby giving you the opportunity to assess the interpersonal skills of these potential supervisors.

Tip 32:
Train Side-by-Side Mentors

A lmost all complete training programs dedicate a portion of the training time to having trainees sit side-by-side with a veteran rep. This standard and important practice allows the trainee to observe and watch the application of what they're being taught in the classroom. As the trainee gains experience, they will take calls with the support of the veteran rep sitting beside them and listening to them. However, too often a new rep is asked to plug in with any available rep, instead of a well-trained and experienced mentor who will be able to demonstrate proper techniques and help smoothly transition the new rep to taking calls.

It's hard to overestimate how much of the real, practical training takes place on the floor working side-by-side with veteran agents, as opposed to studying in the classroom. Trainees, especially if they are just sitting with anyone who may have been available, may hear, "That may be what they teach you in the classroom, but this is how it really works." They may learn shortcuts, observe workarounds, and may even observe bad habits or hear wrong information. They will also learn what is important from a management perspective, as their mentor will inevitably inform them of expectations, things to avoid, important stats, and more.

As we all know, there's a difference between theory and practice, so reps will naturally gravitate to what they perceive as the more practical methods and habits of the side-by-side mentor, as opposed to the methods they were taught in the classroom. This is not unlike learning a foreign language. The language taught in the classroom is usually the "proper" manner of speaking, but when one is conversing with native speakers, shortcuts are taken, slang enters the vocabulary, and grammar rules are routinely ignored. The end result is someone doing very well in the classroom may have trouble communicating in real life situations. In your call center however, while some slang and shortcuts may creep unto the floor, you want new agents to keep to the "proper" and official methods.

Therefore, to ensure the approved classroom techniques align with what the rep hears on the floor, it's important to take time to train those who will serve in the role of side-by-side mentors. This is not a common practice, but will greatly enhance new hire training.

To do this, first, remind the side-by-side trainers what it was like their first days on the floor, and how important it was to receive solid, side-by-side, positive mentorship. Go through the new hire agenda with them, showing them when the trainees will be with them, and what subjects will be covered on each day of the training. Enlist their help in reinforcing information and techniques recently learned. Ask them to avoid using work arounds, and be extra careful in the information they provide to callers.

Daily inform the mentors where the student will be seated, and set an agenda for what tasks the trainee should be doing on each day. As a general rule do not allow the common practice of letting the trainee and side-by-side mentor negotiate what tasks will be done by whom. For example, if the trainee will listen while the veteran takes calls, or will the trainee take calls while the veteran listens in and assists when needed. Instead let the official trainer establish these protocols on a daily basis, either collectively for the entire group, or individually on a trainee-by-trainee basis.

In addition to the training agenda, provide a guideline for the side-by-side mentors. Here is an example:

Day 1: Observation only. The goal today is for the trainee to observe as many calls as possible. Do not offer explanations or elaborate on what you're doing. They will be noting down the type of questions they hear, but not the answers.

Day 2: Further observation. Trainees will play "Call Center Bingo" and "Build a Customer Story" (described in the following tips).

Day 3: Observation, but as time allows ask the trainee if they understand what you're doing, particularly in regard to navigating systems. Take time to explain the resources available to you and how you determine which one to use.

Day 4: By today most trainees should be able to point to where the answer to the caller's question is. They'll be writing down the questions they hear, what they think the answer is, and noting if they knew the answer or where to look for it.

Day 5: Trainees have been practicing navigation in the classroom. As they can, allow them to navigate the systems while you converse with the customer. If they're slowing you down, simply wave them off and take over. After the call is completed go back and explain why you used each system or application.

Day 6: Your trainee has role-played common question types. They should be able to answer calls. Assist them by navigating systems and pointing to information. If they're struggling simply wave them off and interrupt by saying, "Hello Mr. Jones, this is Randy. I'm on the line training with Kelly, and I'd be happy to assist you today."

The trainee has been coached that once you start talking they will immediately stop and remain quite until after the call. After the call is over, please go back and explain what you did and why.

Day 7: Continuation of Day 6.

Days 8 -10: Trainees should be on their own at this point, managing both systems and communicating with callers. Observe and point and assist on the call as necessary. If something needs to be clarified or further explanation given, signal the trainee to put the caller on hold and explain the situation to them so they can relay the information to the customer. If you do not feel they can explain it well, come back from hold with the following, "Hello this is Randy, Chris explained your situation to me and I can help you." While the trainee is taking calls be sure to provide specific, positive feedback when you have the opportunity.

The above mentor guide helps both the mentor and the trainee understand their daily expectations and provides them a daily game plan. You may need to tailor the plan to allow some trainees to stay behind for a day or two to ensure they have grasped all required information before moving forward. Regardless, this guideline will greatly enhance the all-important on-floor portion of training.

Finally, don't forget to regularly connect with the mentors for feedback on the trainees sitting with them. Were they engaged? Are they keeping pace? Do they sound confident on the phone? While you can get this in written form or by surveying the mentors, they often want to give the trainee the benefit of the doubt and tend to be very easy on them with any kind of written evaluation. Experience indicates having a casual conversation with mentors is usually the best way to obtain honest and candid feedback on the progress of the trainees.

Tip 33:
Call Center Bingo

Call Center Bingo is a game I occasionally like to play in the center. Each rep receives a "bingo card" consisting of a 5 x 5 grid. Instead of numbers and letters however, each square is a call type. For example, squares might be "status question" or "payment question." Usually I reserve the free space for the most difficult question or an irate customer. That way if the rep gets an irate caller they are actually happy as it gets them a valuable bingo space. Once a rep gets a bingo, or fills up the card if we are playing "blackout," they receive a prize.

This game works well in a couple scenarios.

For example, when reps first start doing side-by-sides, one of two things often happen that Bingo can help with. One, reps distract the call taker by asking many questions. While this appears helpful at first glance, it reduces the more important objective of allowing them to observe as many calls as possible. Bingo can also help keep the trainee's attention. Without something to focus on, trainees often start to direct their attention elsewhere. Having them mark the card keeps them engaged and thinking about the call.

I also use Call Center Bingo if I start to see call category selection lose accuracy. Proper call category selection is extremely important for your center. Bingo keeps reps focused and thinking about call types, leading to greater accuracy when they are selecting categories or call types in your call tracking system.

Tip 34:
Create a Customer Story

A nother good exercise, particularly during the side-by-side lis-tening portion of new hire training, is to challenge reps to build a complete story about the callers they hear. Have them deduce from the brief conversation any subtle clues and make inferences about the caller. Are they young or old, what type of job do they have, are they married or single, or what type of house do they live in? Of course most of the reasoning is conjecture and not observation. But the accuracy of the report doesn't matter. Having reps involved in the exercise encourages them to listen very closely, and having them listen to the customer closely and completely is a skill you will want to continually help them develop.

Tip 35:
Test Desk During Training

The first day on their own taking calls can be very chaotic and confusing for a rep. A very common problem that is frustrating and wastes new rep's time on their first solo day, as well their supervisor's time, is the issue of getting logged onto all their computer and phone systems.

Don't be fooled into thinking if a rep has signed onto systems in training class that once they get to their new desks for their first day of actual floor work their systems will all be ok. Or since IT has tested the systems they will work for the rep. Usually that's true, but not always. So for one of their shadow or side-by-side times have the rep sign into all their systems and take calls from their new desk, with the mentor rep there, instead of at the mentor desk.

This will ensure:

1. All sign-ones and systems are in working order and ready to go.

2. The rep is familiar with their workstation and environment.

This will go a long way toward creating a smooth initial first day, and allow supervisors to work with reps on customer questions, instead of sign-on or password issues.

Tip 36:
Graduation Tests

In order to graduate from training reps should be required to pass a test consisting of both written and simulated work. The test not only confirms the material has been mastered, but also shows the seriousness and importance of product knowledge. Having a test toward the end of training gives students a deadline by which to know their material. Without a test it's too easy for trainees to coast along and assume they will pick up the information eventually. But with the knowledge of a test looming, students will be more likely to study the material and make sure they know and understand it.

A good format for a new hire training class test is to have three timed sections. Part one consists of items you want reps to be able to say and process without hesitation. These are your Top Ten most common customer questions. When grading these look for simple, clean answers that follow a script as closely as possible. Have the students use a computer to test not only what the student says, but how they process the call.

Part two is comprised of concepts you want reps to be able to reason through. The answer is not as cut and dry as it is from questions in part one. The answers are more nuanced and might bring multiple concepts together. Here you can evaluate if reps understand the training well enough to apply critical thinking skills to what they have learned. I think of these as similar to "word problems" from a high school math assignment.

Part three consists of questions involving the looking up or referencing of information. Here you are testing to see how well reps can use their tools to find an answer. This ranges from the simple of looking up account or order information, to using knowledge databases to find answers to questions they do not know.

Once you have the scores from these three areas, stack the reps in two columns. In the first column stack the reps by the correctness or quality of answers. In the second column stack them by the time it took to complete the test. Reps near the top in both columns are reps with the highest potential, and likely to be your future stars.

In addition to determining who passes out of training and onto the floor, the scores also give future supervisors an indication of how their reps will transition to taking calls. Reps who finish quickly are likely to have lower than average handle times. Some reps may be high in quality but among the last in completion time. Having this information will help your supervisors coach the new reps as they assimilate unto the floor.

While some portions of your graduation tests may be written, have as much of the test as possible simulations or role plays of real customer questions. It's a good practice to have the eventual supervisor come in and participate as the customer when doing role-play tests. It helps the supervisor obtain an understanding of where exactly their new reports are at, and form a plan to address any areas of weakness. Even if there are no areas of weakness, the test gives the supervisor a baseline understanding of the rep's knowledge and comfort levels so they can evaluate individual progress. The tests do not have to be grueling or extensive in order to be valuable and provide this information. But you should be confident if someone has passed the test, they're ready to move to the floor.

Tip 37:
Celebrate Graduation

Successfully learning your company's products and services, and graduating from training is something to celebrate! While having a ceremony to mark and celebrate graduation from a training class is not required, it's a trait common to almost all great training programs. Good trainers recognize celebrations are a way to mark transitions, and moving from a trainee to a new rep on the floor certainly qualifies as such.

A ceremony reinforces to new reps the idea that they've been adequately trained. Knowing they've been trained and prepared for the job gives them the confidence they will need as they begin their call center career. Certificates and cake further validate their understanding of their new position, and help them feel like part of the team.

Tip 38:
Pay Them to Quit

A somewhat radical idea becoming increasingly popular is to end training with an offer to trainees to quit their positions. At the end of training offer reps who have just graduated $1,000 to walk away from the company right now, no questions asked, no problems.

Anyone who takes the money surely wasn't up to the task and most likely was going to cost you a lot more than $1,000 in meetings, re-training, and disciplinary action. Or they were likely already considering leaving as soon as they could find another job, leaving you with an unexpected hole to fill.

But those who stay, which will be more than 98% of your training group, have dedicated themselves to the job and your company. In their mind they have turned down a short-term payout for a career, or at least a long-term commitment. They will hit the floor bonded to you and the company.

Tip 39:
Creating a Smooth Transition to the Floor

As reps transition out of training and start their positions on the floor, they will naturally be less productive than experienced reps. They will notice that some days they seem like they are making progress toward productivity goals, but other days they seem like they might never be able to reach the speed of veteran reps. This can have an effect on their morale as they begin to wonder if they will ever reach required productivity levels. Unfortunately, some reps feeling pressure to take as many phone calls as more experienced reps may begin to cut corners to increase the amount of calls they take. This can lead to bad habits. These bad habits rarely are corrected, because even when their productivity reaches the expected level, they know if they continue to cut the same corners their productivity will be even better.

A way to relieve much of this pressure is to have them slowly assimilate onto the floor through a "Plus One" goal program. Here's how it works. On day one out of training you give each rep a very easy goal of number of calls to take. Maybe if your reps average fifty calls a day, then the new rep's goal is twenty-five. It should be a number they can consider and think, "That's easy, I can do that." Once the new rep reaches that goal they stop taking calls for the remainder of the day. During the remainder of their day they read study materials, or better yet, if possible, they listen to some of the calls they took that day and self-evaluate the calls. Reaching the calls taken goal will give the rep confidence.

The next day when they come in their goal is one additional call, for a total of twenty-six. Since it's only one more than the prior day it seems easy to reach. And it should be. Once they reach the goal, again they listen to calls they took that day for self-evaluation, or if that's not possible they do self-study, or maybe sit and observe an experienced rep. Their confidence grows by meeting their daily, productivity goal.

This process continues each day. If they do not reach their goal, whatever number they do reach becomes their baseline and the next day their goal is their new baseline plus one. So if the goal for the day was 42 and the rep answered 31, their goal is back down to 32. The thought of "climbing the ladder," as we like to call it, becomes a fun game in itself. The reps cheer each other on as the try to reach the top of the ladder. Once they reach the eventual goal, which I suggest setting at 90% of the average calls of an experienced rep, they have completed the final phase of training and assume normal production goals. Now instead of the normal trepidation and insecurity of a new rep, they hit the floor with confidence knowing they're ready to perform at the same level as their peers.

Tip 40:
Starter Responses

A common complaint of customers is they are sent "canned re- sponses" that at worst don't specifically answer their questions, and at best answer the question but leave the customer feeling they have not experienced an even basic level of personal service. Man- agers however, encourage canned responses to increase rep stats and productivity, and know using pre-written responses will result in more consistent answers with better grammar and correct spelling.

The answer to keeping agent productivity high without your custom- ers feeling like they're getting canned responses is to *start* with a canned, or template, response, but then *personalize* the answer. This is often more difficult than it sounds, but there are ways to achieve the right balance.

1) Instead of calling canned responses "canned responses," call them "starter responses." This helps cement in the agent's mind they need to make modifications and personalize the templates they use. If an agent thinks an email response is set in stone and they can't or shouldn't improve on it, they won't. But if they realize that the standard response is simply a starting point, they'll understand they need to tailor their email reply to fit the customer's needs. As a result, agents will also look more closely at the customer's email and will be more likely to give a complete response that answers the exact question.

2) Provide a set of standard phrases rather than complete re- sponses. The agent will then be required to go in and com- plete certain important pieces of information. This is more productive than free writing, but at the same time requires the

reps to interact with the email, ensuring a more personal response.

When you use starter responses instead of canned responses, you may slightly lower productivity, but you'll make up for it with improved quality scores and higher first time resolution rates.

Tip 41:
Have Off-Line Support Agents Take Calls

It's a best practice to specifically select and train email and chat reps for those off-line channels. But while their training may be focused on these channels and skills geared toward them, it's also important to have off-line support reps take calls soon after leaving training, or as part of their training. But I don't mean a couple here or there. I mean for a long enough time for them to be very comfortable on the phone and reach productivity levels of full time phone reps.

The experience of taking calls helps email/ chat reps reach their productivity potential. I have seen this many times. An email rep trained specifically on email eventually reaches a productivity plateau. Then they are put on the phone for a few weeks, and when they return to email their productivity is increased fifteen or twenty percent. The reason is talking with a customer on the phone provides the reps with immediate feedback. Reps learn what customers *mean* when they ask a question, beyond just what they specifically *say*. When answering email if a customer phrases something a particular way you may not know exactly what information they are looking for and have to take a guess. You won't know until they reply hours later if you were correct. Even then, the email reply may go to another rep, so the rep who sent the original reply has no idea if they were able to provide the customer with the information they needed. However when the rep is on the phone, the caller gives immediate feedback if the rep response doesn't answer their *intended* question, and so the rep is then able to provide the actual information the customer needs. In this way the rep learns the vocabulary of the customer. The rep also learns what follow up questions are likely to come next. Through these two-way exchanges with customers, reps gain a clearer understanding of customer needs and questions behind the question, which is something they cannot achieve solely by answering email. However, once they have this understanding they can return to email and apply it to emails they answer. They now become much more efficient and provide higher quality answers.

In addition, being on the phone increases the speed reps are able to achieve using internal systems. When only doing email there is not the time pressure to manipulate systems quickly, and as a result, reps again tend to reach a plateau. But the pressure of having a caller on the phone waiting for the rep motivates the rep to increase their ability to access information quickly, leading to higher productivity when they go back to working on email.

Tip 42:
The First Eight Seconds

As part of your customer service skills training, emphasize the first eight seconds of the call. The call opening sets the tone and often defines the customer's experience for the entire call. A really good opening conveys to the customer the rep cares and is willing to help. If the rep gets this right, the caller will often give them the benefit of the doubt and more leeway if the rest of the call becomes more difficult, or the rep struggles to find information the customer requests.

The tone and enthusiasm with which the rep answers the phone is key. A flat tone conveys disinterest and lack of willingness to help, while an enthusiastic greeting creates an immediate positive impression.

Another important aspect of the opening is to take any suspense out of the call as soon as possible. When customers call, they are often unsure if they're going to receive their desired service resolution. They may even assume they will need to argue with the rep or a supervisor to get their problem resolved. This often results in the customer being in an irate or elevated emotional state that will not change until they hear a resolution that will satisfy them. Agents should be trained to take the suspense out of the call as soon as they know they can help the customer.

For example, consider the following scenario: Ms. Lewis has been traveling for weeks. She returns home and opens an item sent from your company. Unfortunately, it's not quite right and Ms. Lewis would like to make an exchange. She goes to your website and reads all exchanges must be requested within thirty days. However, it's been thirty-five days since the purchase date.

Ms. Lewis calls your center, and as she dials the phone she mentally prepares herself to argue for the right of an extension. She may assume she's going to be told, "Thirty days is our policy—sorry, there is nothing we can do." She assumes she will then need to demand to speak to a supervisor and is preparing herself to continue to escalate until she is able to make the exchange.

She does not know however, that while you state a thirty-day policy on the website, reps have been given the authority to immediately approve an exchange for up to forty-five days after the purchase date.

Here's the wrong way to handle the call. When Ms. Lewis calls and requests for the exemption to the thirty-day policy, the agent does not immediately respond with any indication of resolution, but instead with "Just a moment please…." Then the agent asks for order information, then brings up the order to examine it, then authenticates the customer—all before letting Ms. Lewis know they will be able to resolve the situation to her satisfaction. Ms. Lewis therefore remains agitated and on the defensive during the two to three minutes of look up and authentication process, as it's not clear if she will receive a refund or a "sorry that's our policy" response.

Compare this opening with the agent immediately leading with, "Certainly, Ms. Lewis if you purchased the item thirty-five days ago I'll be very happy to process your exchange. May I please have your order number?"

With this phrasing the customer will calm down right away. Notice how the rep didn't promise anything; they only confirmed that if what the customer said was true, than they would be able to make the exchange or refund. This allows some room in case what the customer stated is actually not correct, and the rep may have to deliver bad news.

Keys to the opening are letting the customers know right away they have reached someone who can help them, and for the rep to take the suspense out of the call. Answering every call with an enthusiastic tone, as well as these components, should be emphasized early and strongly throughout training and on an ongoing basis.

Tip 43:
Every Call Counts

It's common for reps to deflect constructive criticism of a call they handled poorly by saying, "I just had one bad call; give me a break." If you hear this, a simple way to get the conversation to a less defensive place is to ask the rep how many bad calls they should be allowed to have in a day. Usually, this answer will make the point you expect every call to be handled with the utmost of professionalism.

A good illustration to help cement this idea is to compare CSRs to actors. Ask reps to think about themselves as stage performers. Whenever they pick up the phone they're on stage and the customer deserves their full effort and attention. The caller paid for his ticket by waiting in the queue, and is entitled to see a good show.

Ask reps not to take the next call if they aren't in the right state of mind. Allow reps to take the occasional quick break or walk around the building if they need it to mentally prepare themselves for the next call. But let them know once they return to their desk and put themselves into available for that next call, they're on the hook to deliver their lines, and provide the caller with their best performance.

Tip 44:
Don't Let Customers Vent

One of the most important skills for a CSR to master is handling difficult or irate callers. Doing so will increase a rep's confidence, lower their stress, reduce the amount of transfers they need to make to supervisors, as well as improve the experience of those who call in upset. Despite all these benefits, most call centers consider handling difficult callers to be an optional class, or at least one that's near the bottom of the priority list. But if you want to run a best-in-class service operation, you'll need to invest the time and energy to train in this critical area.

And here's something every rep needs to know and internalize: the angriest customer is the one who has the potential to become your very best friend. Customers who are angry at you are the ones who had high expectations. They really wanted to believe that their experience with your company would be positive. They tend to live in a world of extremes: either you're a friend or an enemy. And when they call and unleash their emotions, you have the opportunity to become their friend. You have the opportunity to create a situation where the customer hangs up after the call and says to themselves—and to anyone else within earshot—"That was a very pleasant surprise!"

Perhaps the most important aspect of the difficult customer interaction is to move the conversation off the problem and onto the solution as quickly as possible.

Once, shortly after taking charge of a new center I walked by a workstation to see a rep with his head down, and I could hear an elevated voice coming through his headset. I asked the rep what was happening. He looked up while muting the line and said, "Oh, I'm letting the customer vent." I asked the rep to give me the headset. I interrupted the customer and introduced myself. After telling the customer that I understood how they felt, I quickly offered an acceptable resolution to the issue. The customer was satisfied and quickly began telling me how great our service was! Contrast my experience with the rep who was listening to the customer go on and on and feeling browbeaten by the customer.

I have found one of the most important and effective strategies in dealing with irate callers is to *not* heed the long-accepted advice to "let them vent." I'm not sure how letting callers go on and on railing to reps became such iconic wisdom in the call center world. I do know this however: If you let a caller continue to vent their frustration without a positive response, they'll become increasingly worked up and may begin to make demands you're not able to meet. Further, your reps will grow weary and burned out by having to listen to customers complain, and unmercifully belittle both your company and them.

A more effective strategy in helping an extremely frustrated customer is to move off the problem and onto the solution as quickly as possible. This essential strategy should be taught and drilled with reps extensively. Usually it's as simple as saying, "I understand your frustration. I do not consider this acceptable either. Let me do this for you," and then provide an appropriate solution.

To be clear, I'm not trying to imply you should not let the customer explain the situation. What I'm proposing is that you train reps to *listen* to the customer's problem, *empathize* with the situation, *reassure* the customer you do not consider what happened acceptable, and then as quickly as possible *inform* them of a possible resolution.

By doing so, you have a good chance of converting an irate caller into a loyal customer.

Tip 45:
Teach a Grammar Class

We sometimes assume when we hire an intelligent, articulate person, he or she already possess good writing skills, especially if the person is a college student or graduate. But if you want effective, well-written emails, don't assume this is the case. Too often you'll find reps lack the business writing skills you assume they have.

To resolve this simply take the time to train them yourself. Incorporate a business writing and grammar module into your training curriculum. Teach basic sentence structure, how to write clear concise sentences, words to avoid, basic grammar, and other writing tips. The time you spend as an English teacher will pay off greatly by reducing the time you spend as the grader of their written communication.

Tip 46:
60/30/15-Minute Modules

Due to the unpredictable nature of the call center, you'll occasionally find yourself with high rep available times. Ideally, you can use these times for ongoing training. However, if you have to take the time to talk to your trainer, decide on an appropriate subject, and ask him or her to prepare something, by the time the trainer is ready to go to work the center will inevitably be busy again and the opportunity to train is lost.

A solution is to have ongoing training modules ready at a moment's notice. Then, whenever you find yourself with time, you can pull out a module and began training.

Have trainers create fifteen-, thirty-, and sixty-minute modules. Then depending on how long the slow period will last, ask them to pick an appropriate one and start training.

This is especially useful if systems go down and are expected to be up soon. Rather than have everyone sit around and chat, announce "quick training" and have trainers deliver a short, fifteen-minute, in-the-aisle training module. Do it in the aisle to save the time it takes everyone to get to the training room, and because when the systems come back up you'll need to stop the training and have everyone resume taking calls as quickly as possible.

Obviously, the type of training appropriate for this spur of the moment activity is not information reps need to do their job on a daily basis. This works well with customer skills brush-up training, which is always good to talk about on an ongoing basis, no matter how much time you spent on it during new hire training. Other good examples of module topics include handling escalations, rare call types, how to stay motivated, and so on.

Tip 47:
The One-Page Cheat Sheet

A great job aid for any new rep is to create and hand them a laminated, 8 ½ by 11 cheat sheet crammed with as much information as possible. While it is true most of the same information you'll put on the card is available to the rep on your intranet, or in their new hire training manual, the card will be the easiest and fastest way for reps to get the information while on the phone. Even though you would like to go paperless, if you want new reps to be as efficient as possible, a one-pager is the way to go.

In order to cram as much information on the cheat sheet as possible, utilize every possible space on the both sides of the card. Create outlined sections written in small font and even sideways to maximize the amount of information on the card.

Handy websites, phone numbers, internal codes, abbreviations, quick scripts, and popular FAQs can be placed on the cards. Continue to add information until the card is full, box in sections, and do not be afraid to squeeze information in horizontally, vertically, or wherever it will fit. Use both sides and laminate in order to create a more complete and lasting copy.

Tip 48:
Training a Group by Listening to Calls

Calibration is the process of having a group listen to and score calls together. This helps ensure consistency in your internal quality monitor scoring process, and is essential for achieving consistency among the quality assurance staff, supervisors, or other personnel that may provide quality review by scoring phone calls or emails.

But listening to calls in a group setting is not only important for consistency in call scoring; it also can be an effective and powerful part of your new and ongoing rep training. Having reps listen to others provides them with the opportunity to hear other's techniques and learn from them, and to give and receive constructive feedback with peers.

In order for call listening to be an effective training tool though, reps need to be comfortable listening to other's recorded calls. If they're not comfortable in this setting the opportunity for learning is minimized. Instead of listening and appreciating the feedback, the rep may be thinking of responses to criticism they fear they're about to receive. But if the reps are used to the idea and it's an established part of the center's culture, this is a very effective method of ongoing feedback and training, and can serve as either a staff meeting agenda item, or as a complete training meeting.

They key to doing this training well is the meeting leader. In addition to being careful to provide effective feedback in a positive manner, the leader must be able to lead the group in doing so as well.

When conducting these sessions have the leader start with a positive question, such as, "What do we *like* about this call?"

If, after a slight pause of silence, someone responds with a fairly generic answer such as, "She was really polite," or "I thought he had a good tone," the leader can dig deeper.

But then someone might quickly say, "She forgot the offer of future assistance." Then someone else will say, "He could have offered to do this or that." When this happens it's important the meeting leader immediately steer back to the positive, otherwise you'll be left with the not-so-favorable ratio of one generic positive comment to many criticisms disguised as constructive feedback. This can be deflating to the rep who took the call, and invoke a reflexive, defensive response that may minimize their potential to learn from the call. Fully exhaust specific, positive aspects of the call before going on to opportunities for improvement.

When it's time to turn the group's attention to the negative aspects, it's very important the language used does not invoke a defensive reaction. For example, instead of "What should they have done?" say instead, "What could they do differently next time?" If there's something egregious on the call, stop focusing on the call and instead focus on the situation. "We encountered a difficult situation here, how would you have handled it?" Ask them to role-play the scenario. In these cases, leave the specific call for individual coaching and instead create a learning opportunity for the group that no longer focuses on the specific call. Again, the purpose in these meetings is not discipline—it's learning. If the call brings up a case where discipline or further action is required, take that offline to be dealt with on an individual basis.

Also, the idea of scoring in front of each other creates a certain amount of competitive focus and potential for embarrassment, both of which can detract from the more pure aspects of simply observing and learning. Therefore, carefully consider if you want to simply listen to the calls for feedback, or if you need to score them. When the purpose of the calibration is consistent scoring amongst QA staff, obviously calls need to be scored. But when the purpose of the group listening session is to teach and help reps improve, all the benefits can be achieved without the potential embarrassment of an actual score.

Section III
Managing Your Call Center

Management is the practice of directing and encouraging the people who work for you. In the call center you have a heavy population of entry level workers who will create many challenges for you and your management staff. But if you can succeed in creating a dynamic, positive culture in which agents can grow and thrive in their careers, you'll find your employees will go the extra mile for your customers.

In most companies the call center has more statistics regarding their staff than any other department in the corporation. While most departments struggle with having reliable productivity measurements, if anything the customer service department struggles with having too much data regarding employees. With all this information, it's important to keep in mind what all the statistics are actually telling you about your agents. In addition, it's critical to establish a culture where reps do not feel they're managed just by the numbers. Most importantly, you want your management team to understand that numbers are rarely the full story; they're simply a great indicator of where they should focus attention. Many of the tips in this chapter aim to help you get beyond the numbers.

Tip 49:
Create a Culture of Learning

Learning + Enjoyment = Performance

The above formula may seem a little simplistic or even trite. However, most people would agree that happy, motivated employees will perform best. Employee engagement and happiness is critical in customer facing roles. If a rep is in a bad mood, or unhappy in their job, it will inevitably show up in the service they provide to customers. It's very difficult for an unhappy employee to be able to answer the phone with a positive tone and with the requisite enthusiasm needed to handle difficult customer interactions.

Creating a culture of learning is one of the best ways to guard against burnout, and creating a positive culture makes your center a better place to work and leads to better performance. When employees are learning and their minds are active they're in a higher state of awareness, and more likely to have genuine enthusiasm when they interact with customers. As a call center leader you should always be looking for ways to encourage agents to learn.

The subject matter is not always important. In great centers agents are often given learning opportunities basically irrelevant to the jobs they're performing. If it leads to a better employee experience, ultimately this will benefit customers, even if the subjects are unrelated to the rep's job. The goal is not always to teach reps direct skills to improve in their performance (although of course that's important); the goal is to create an environment people want to be a part of. If they like the company, if they like their co-workers, and if they like the opportunities they're given to learn, they'll inevitably display a positive attitude when talking or interacting with customers. To the extent you can create an enjoyable work experience, your reps will be in a positive mood when talking with customers, and this will lead to improved satisfaction results. It will also lower expense by lowering attrition and associated training costs.

Creating learning opportunities and fun activates can be time consuming and often requires an investment. I recommend budgeting a set amount per rep per month for employee welfare—for most centers, around $30 per agent per month. Having these funds budgeted in advance will provide freedom to spend money when the time comes, without having to worry about the expense, as it's already planned and accounted for.

In regards to creating fun activities, often forming a steering committee made of call center staff, including reps, is a great way to both relieve some of this burden from you and get more employees involved in the process. A "culture steering committee" can help establish programs that often have greater buy in and participation amongst staff than programs coming from managers. The committee can also serve as a creative outlet for employees who like to plan parties and is a development opportunity for them. I've found that even when given a small budget, cultural committees can accomplish a great deal. Also, I know some managers fear this type of employee empowerment may lead to extravagance or other issues, but in reality I find activities planned by a group of staff often are less expensive, and more conservative in nature than those planned by official corporate entities.

Tip 50:
Manage by Walking Around

Y ou can learn much of what you need to know about your call center by walking the aisles. The simple act of walking around and talking with reps leads to an incredible amount of important discoveries—which reps are performing well, which ones aren't motivated, what the current challenges are in the center, what the current customer complaints are, and what frustrations reps are feeling when trying to do their job. A goal I set for all my managers is to know more about their people than I do. But I continually shock them by telling them which reps are having difficulty, which reps are having personal problems, and which reps need someone to pat them on the back.

Managers always ask how I know this. I know because I take ten minutes out of every day to walk around, talk with reps, and get to know them. Not only does this lead me to understand what's going on in the center, but it also helps develop a level of trust so when problems or issues occur, reps are comfortable talking with me. This is the most profitable *and* the most enjoyable ten minutes of my day.

It's very low key—I mostly say "hello" and put a face to the name behind my title. But I also take this opportunity to ask reps about how they're feeling, what customers are saying, and how they feel about certain initiatives within the center. I ask them about their personal statistics, call monitoring reviews, or comfort level with the amount of training they have received regarding new products or services. As a result I'm able to form a realistic impression of how reps feel about their job, their supervisor, and the programs we roll out in an effort to improve the center. Managers who don't make this time are trading a few minutes for hours later when they have to dig through employee dissatisfaction and other issues that could have been easily dealt with if discovered early on.

Informal learning from walking the floor applies to customer issues as well. Being on the floor provides feedback from your customers and allows you to make necessary changes and course corrections in virtual real-time. It might take hours or even days for customer feedback to reach you through reports or escalations, but a quick trip to the floor and a brief conversation with the reps will usually tell you what problems your customers are currently experiencing, allowing you to get a quick start on a resolution, preventing potential calls and heading off customer dissatisfaction.

Tip 51:
Allow Reps to Listen to Themselves

One of the most effective, if not *the* most effective, actions a manager can take to improve the quality of customer interactions in their center is to allow reps to listen to themselves. Nothing is more powerful than actually hearing the words we say and how we say them, and nothing changes rep behavior faster than the simple process of listening to themselves.

Allowing the reps to listen to themselves is far more powerful and leads to better results than the feedback from their supervisor or a quality analyst. Consider a supervisor who goes up to an agent and says, "You need to improve your tone." Without context the rep can do little to internalize this feedback and use it to improve. Contrast this feedback with a rep and a supervisor listening to a call together, and before the supervisor begins to coach or offer feedback, the rep provides his own feedback based on what he heard on the call. The rep is internalizing this self-provided feedback. The supervisor should serve as a guide to point the rep to where and what to listen to.

Having reps listen to themselves is so powerful it's effective even when there's no one to guide the rep, and they simply listen to themselves without any coaching or feedback. In fact, I often wonder if many centers would be better off if they did away with their internal QA teams and simply allowed reps to listen to their prior days' calls for thirty minutes a day. Also, allowing reps the opportunity to listen to themselves without management feedback is a great transition step for centers implementing quality programs for the first time, and reps are apprehensive about having their calls monitored and reviewed.

If you're going to have reps listen to themselves without the guidance of a supervisor or monitor, I recommend you have them write down and turn in answers to these three basic questions:

1) What was the call about?

2) What did I do that should be considered a best practice?

3) What do I want to do differently next time?

The answers to these questions are not important. The goal is for the rep to listen to the call openly. If they do, and they have a desire to improve, inevitably they will. When you have reps listen to themselves without the supervisor or quality coach, you've removed the pressure usually felt by reps and left them free to learn without the natural defensiveness that often accompanies a call review session. Without any defensiveness, the rep can concentrate fully on improving their skills.

Tip 52:
Productivity Measures

As ACD systems began to be rolled out, they offered a wide variety of statistics previously unavailable to managers. At first, most managers focused on the number of calls reps had taken, rewarding reps most productive by this measure. While this was commonplace, and still is to some extent, incenting the number of calls taken per rep inevitably pressures the rep to hurry through calls as quickly as possible.

This can lead to a number of issues. First, when reps know they will be judged on the basis of how many calls they take, they are motivated to take shortcuts and do everything in their power to keep customer conversations as brief as possible. Often this means the customer loses by not having their questions fully answered. The customer may even have to call back, creating additional contacts, and costing the center money in the long run.

This is also inequity in judging reps by the number of calls they take. Some reps may work on busier shifts, or may work during a time when phone calls tend to be brief, giving these reps a distinct advantage over those on other shifts.

Additionally, if the rewards or penalties are strong enough, there is the possibility reps may cut customers off, or take other unfavorable actions to improve their stats.

If you need your reps to increase their productivity, there's a much better way. John Wooden, the famous UCLA basketball coach, once said he never talked about winning; he only talked about doing those things that *led to winning*. It's the same thing with phone calls: If you emphasize positive metrics such as keeping wrap-up times short and being available to take calls, reps who statistically do well in those categories will also end up taking the most phone calls, but without the negative effects that tend to happen when taking a high amount of calls is directly emphasized and rewarded.

Because of the danger in managing by the number of calls taken, most centers have done away with managing by this number and now manage by average handle time (or AHT). AHT is comprised of talk time + hold time + wrap up time. While this approach is slightly more enlightened, it also has its dangers and drawbacks. If you measure agents based on this number they will do everything in their power to lower their AHT, but many of their actions may not lead to higher productivity, and may in fact lead to decreased quality of customer interactions.

One issue is that reps usually translate AHT to talk time. They do not necessarily understand there are multiple ways to lower AHT, so they focus on the most obvious and highest one: talk time. This is the worst possible case for the customer. The rep is now thinking any deviation from a fast resolution will negatively impact them. They are not incented to spend the time to resolve complex issues, or probe to ensure they fully understand the issue.

One way to alleviate this pressure is to judge productivity solely at the team or supervisor level. Centers using this approach do not talk to individual agents about AHT, but the supervisors are measured by their teams AHT. Therefore, if an agent has high AHT, the supervisor must go and begin to work with the agent, and find ways to help them reduce the AHT. Usually this is accomplished by working with the agent side-by-side and coaching them on systems, process, or product knowledge. In this scenario the agent continues to focus on quality, but is also coached on ways to become more efficient. This will lead to lower AHT and more calls taken in a day, without the potential negative side effects that may occur when the rep is measured on AHT directly. It also incents supervisors to look at process issues that lead to higher AHT.

For example, I once worked with a supervisor who was attempting to lower her team's AHT. We observed all the leads were stationed at one side of the room, and the process for a rep with a question was to go speak with the lead directly. We were able to lower the hold time by simply dispersing leads throughout the center so rep travel time was decreased. Because the supervisor was looking at this as a team problem not an individual one, the solution was more universal and holistic than if she were working on each individual's AHT.

In terms of a rep measure for productivity, the method I recommend is judging productivity on the combination of time spent talking + time spent in available waiting for an incoming call. In this framework there is no difference between talking and being in available, so reps are never incented to hurry through a call. They are only incented once they get off a call to get back into available as soon as possible. I refer to this as "willing time," since the agent was either on a call or willing to be on one. I have found this is a strong incentive to reduce wrap up time and be more efficient, without potential negative effects of looking at call handling averages or gross number of calls taken.

Tip 53:
Performance Documentation

Becoming good at documenting is an important skill for anyone in a management position. However, it's especially critical for the manager of a call center. Because you're dealing with so many entry-level employees, you, unfortunately, will have many opportunities to practice disciplinary management. Inevitably, you'll be forced to terminate a high number of employees. You'll find this process becomes much simpler, and it's much easier to work with your human resources department, if you have learned to document well.

Many managers, especially those with less experience, are continually frustrated because they assume they have provided adequate documentation to terminate employees who, for one reason or another, were not meeting company standards. However, human resources, in their role to protect the company, often requires additional documentation, and further opportunities for the employee to change their behavior. Eventually, managers learn that every comment made to a rep about performance has to be documented in such a way it can be referred to in the future. The easiest way to do this is to simply email yourself a quick note to use as potential future references whenever you have a conversation with an employee about their behavior, even if the conversation is short and the email only contains a sentence or two. You'll save yourself a lot of time and a lot of frustration with the disciplinary process by simply learning to document every conversation you have via a quick e-mail.

If you find you're actually reaching the point of disciplinary action, you may want to copy your human resources department or, in some cases, the employees themselves to document the behavior or the conversation. Copying the employee on an email follow up to a conversation is a solid reinforcement mechanism to show the rep their seriousness of the situation. Anything you can do that will cut down the amount of time it takes to terminate a poor performer will be of immense benefit to you and to your customers.

Use this method of emailing yourself to keep a file for effective reviews as well. While most managers keep files of past annual reviews, tests, training logs, and any disciplinary forms they may have filled out, the file often lacks notes about positive feedback, minor lapses in judgment, or other items that would be useful for future reviews. These email notes will remind you of actions, both good and bad, that took place over the past review period. During review time, if you noted a variety of examples of great rep behavior over the past year, that person will be amazed and impressed you can remember these items. They'll be motivated to continue to do these in the future, providing you with more good things to write down for the next review.

Tip 54:
Managing Punctuality

Punctuality is one of the biggest issues facing every call center, and for most, it's the number one cause of terminations. There are many strategies you can employ to avoid the cycle of punctuality verbal warning, written warning, final warning, and termination—a path all too familiar to most call center mangers.

One, be sure reps understand the importance of being on time. For many positions in companies today start times are flexible. However, in the call center it's not. To emphasize the point when discussing punctuality with a rep, suddenly pause for one full minute. Do not break the inevitable awkward silence for the full minute. Then explain this is the amount of time a customer is holding "for only one minute while waiting for you to arrive for your shift."

Another concept to explain to reps is the compounding effect of "one minute." You can explain this with the following:

"Imagine if calls came in exactly five minutes apart starting at the top of the hour. A rep can handle twelve calls an hour and none of them have to wait. But if you were just *one minute* late, each call would have to wait one minute. Therefore the one minute you're late has resulting in one minute for every caller, for a total of twelve minutes of hold time. And this continues to compound throughout the entire day."

The most effective method of addressing punctuality I have ever used is to cover the rep's tardiness yourself. If a rep is late simply go over to their seat, sit down, sign on to their computer, and begin taking calls. When they show up and see you working in their seat, the rep (1) obviously knows punctuality is important to you, and (2) realizes the extent of your seriousness. When the rep arrives, just shrug and say, "Oh you're here—great," and then return to your office. Within the next fifteen minutes, you'll probably receive an explanation and an apology, and you'll have an employee who knows how visible their tardiness is.

Of course, eventually you have to deal with chronic punctuality issues in the traditional way of documenting, probation, and eventually termination. But a few creative solutions early on in a rep's employment can often turn around a bad habit of being late, and head off the issue before it gets to the stages of disciplinary action.

Tip 55:
Don't Coddle Poor Performers

A common mistake of service center managers is to go too far in encouraging poor performers to work harder, and continue to encourage them to give their best effort in hopes of turning their performance around. Don't get me wrong—I strongly advocate creating a positive, encouraging culture, and I believe everyone should be given the chance to be successful. But at times the kindest and most supportive action a supervisor can take for an employee is to encourage them to find a position more suited to their skills. Remember, the service environment isn't for everyone. The sooner you can move someone whose skills are not suited for the call center to another position, the better it is for both you *and* the employee.

I'm not talking about new employees, or ones with potential who are just struggling a bit over one concept or aspect of their position. I'm referring to those you're able to identify (and usually you can identify them soon after training) whose particular skill set is simply not a good match for a customer service position.

The truth is that generally if you have a poor performing rep who does not have a lot of potential, if you continue to give them an inordinate amount of your time and attention you can prop them up and eventually help them improve to the point where their performance moves from poor to mediocre, and they no longer are performing so poorly you need to terminate them. But now you have a mediocre rep with limited potential. Is that what you want? Are you, your customers, or the rep now better off? Of course the answer is "no."

Unfortunately most managers spend 80% of their time working with the bottom 20% of their reps. Imagine instead if you quickly moved out poor performers to either different positions or out of the company altogether. Now you can spend 80% of your time with the good reps, and have the opportunity to help them grow into great reps!

If a rep is simply not well suited for the position, it is not good for them to continue to remain in a stressful position for which they are not well skilled. It is better for them to find a position that rewards the skills they do have, a position where they will ultimately be more successful and happy. Working with someone to find another position or showing them how a call center position does not fit their skillset is probably the kindest thing a supervisor can do for some reps, even though that may mean an uncomfortable situation in the short term.

Move out poor performers quickly and spend your time with good reps. This will improve the service you offer, and reduce your stress and the stress of those around you.

Tip 56:
Push Stats That Are Important

Many call centers today utilize a reporting portal where supervisors and agents can log into to see their stats. I've been in quite a few centers where the manager has proudly announced, "We're 'paperless,' everything is available online." However, when I ask agents how many calls they took yesterday, or any other common call center statistic, rarely do they know. Even though there will be some exceptions, generally whenever you rely on agents to "pull" the data by going out and accessing it themselves, the statistics become less visible, and not widely utilized, or utilized only by the best reps.

On the other hand, if reps receive a report on their desk every morning with a particular statistic highlighted, that information drives their behavior as they know exactly what to focus on. For example, if the day before an expected heavy volume day you put a sheet on everyone's desk that focuses on productivity stats or goals, you'll see immediate improvement and you can increase productivity for your expected heavy volume day. Reps respond to what you emphasize. Statistics they need to go out and "pull" themselves do not show emphasis. They will recognize and respond to statistics you highlight and "push" to them every day.

Pushing stats is another great way of correcting behavior without the need of formal, disciplinary discussions. Done right, this often leads to improvement in as little as three days.

Here's how it works using the example of improving wrap-up time:

- Day 1: Pass out the report with wrap-up time highlighted.

- Day 2: Hand out the same report. If wrap-up time has improved, next to the rep's name write something like "Better ☺".

- Day 3: Rep shows further improvement, highlight with "Excellent, keep up the great work!"

The employee is happy, motivated, and improving. Contrast this with bringing someone into your office and starting with, "I need to talk to you about your wrap-up time." That's a conversation that increases stress and leads to defensiveness rather than improvement.

Tip 57:
Talk Times

Talk time is a particularly tricky statistic to manage. Is having a lower talk time a sign a rep is more efficient? Or very knowledgeable and so rarely has to put a customer on hold? Or is it an indication the rep tends to cut off conversations early, and does not fully address customer concern? Any of these is possible. The key to managing talk time is to go investigate the outliers whose numbers vary most from the statistical mean. In some cases you'll find agents who need coaching and a change in behavior. In other cases you'll find best practices you'll want to train other agents to emulate. Don't assume the reps with the highest or lowest handle times are doing best or worse. Instead go sit with agents at the top and bottom of the statistical curve and base your judgments on these observations, not the raw numbers.

With new agents a long talk time usually indicates they're placing callers on hold and searching for answers. Over time, as there is less need to place callers on hold, their talk time begins to fall. Then, as the rep becomes more comfortable on the phone and offers more thorough explanations, no longer shying away from potentially difficult situations, their talk time begins to rise and then levels off. At this point they're in their optimal talk time. If this number begins to fall, they may be experiencing burnout and are no longer offering as complete explanations. When talk time begins to drop for experienced reps it's important to investigate for burnout and take steps to help them regain their focus.

While in their optimal zone, some agents naturally achieve higher talk times than others. But again, this is not necessarily good or bad. If someone has a talk time at the upper or lower end of the center, someone should sit side-by-side with them to understand why before drawing conclusions.

Tip 58:
Book of the Month Club

A great way to contribute to a learning culture is to create a book of the month club. Having a book of the month club keeps reps engaged and learning. Here are a few ideas for starting an effective book of the month club:

First, let everyone know there are books available to either own or borrow. This can be done with either a "library," where books are read and returned, or just give the books away. (This is the method I prefer as it tends to be a great motivator to participate). Another idea is to give away the complete set once a year after reading has been concluded, or have a library for the first books, which a lot of reps might read, but start to give them away as reps get further into the program and participation tends to drop. A final option is to offer a cash incentive. To reps who read all twelve of my book of the month club books, I often give a $100 gift certificate to an online bookstore.

When beginning your club, start with motivational books rather than call center or business books. Reps can use these books to create personal goals (including reading their way through the book of the month club). After a motivational book or two, move to general business books, and then finally books on your industry or on the call center industry. I suggest you allow reps to start the program at any time with the month one selection, and when they complete all twelve receive some type of reward.

You can also use a book of the month club as a way to pre-qualify those who want to get into management positions. At some call centers reps are not eligible to apply for a supervisor position until they have read a set curriculum. Having the curriculum not only provides a baseline of understanding based on the books, but also weeds out potential candidates who are not dedicated enough to read a few books.

Tip 59:
Useful Feedback on Customer Contacts

When coaching representatives on their phone calls, I have often heard supervisors making comments such as, "Use a more effective word choice." Or, "You could do a better job," or "You could have been more articulate or clear."

Whenever I hear this, I wonder how I would react if someone said that to me. I am not sure how I could use that to do things differently on my next call. It's not that the feedback is not accurate; it's just that it's not helpful. A far more effective method of coaching is to always provide an acceptable alternative when suggesting the rep needs to improve or change their word choice. While it takes more time, it's far more effective to actually role-play the phone call or rewrite the email and ask reps if they can hear or see the difference than to simply say do better next time.

When given a constructive alternative, reps begin to understand exactly what you're looking for and will no longer be forced to guess or assume what a more appropriate word choice would have been. While individual coaching sessions take longer using this methodology, the results of the improved service and better word choices will come quickly. Incorporate this into your and your supervisors' coaching methods and you'll begin to see improvements.

Tip 60:
The Eye-Roller

A common problem in the call center when kicking off a new incentive plan or initiative, is the one person who sabotages the new idea or program with a bad attitude. I'm not discussing employees who always have a bad attitude, are cancerous to the call center, and need to be dealt with by disciplinary action before their attitudes permeate the whole center. Rather, I'm referring to employees who usually have a good attitude while doing their work, but find your attempts to motivate your team silly or hokey.

If you see buy-in and enthusiasm from the majority of the group, and the "bad apple" makes a sarcastic comment or rolls his or her eyes, this often leads others to view your idea in a negative light. Not surprisingly, it's usually the same one or two people who continually interject negative chemistry into meetings. Of course you can attempt to discipline this person, but it's difficult to define a bad attitude and its negative effects to the extent to take disciplinary action. Besides, this individual may be a good employee but just doesn't like to participate in incentives or other programs that, for whatever reason, they feel are beneath them.

An effective way to deal with this problem is to attack it head on and proactively. Take the individual aside *before* the meeting and discuss what's about to take place. Tell them what you're planning to roll out and acknowledge you know they may consider this to be somewhat hokey. Then, offer them this deal: If they agree to keep a positive attitude, or at least pretend to have one, you will not call upon them or ask them to participate in a way they might consider uncomfortable. Whenever I have made someone this deal, meetings have gone smoothly and without negative disruption. A further benefit is the negative person soon recognizes they have been a disruption and begins to change their attitude. In my experience, after receiving this feedback they often become an active and willing participant in your meetings and incentive plans.

Tip 61:
Elective Training Classes

A nother way to foster a learning culture is to offer elective training classes. Elective training courses are classes reps are free to participate in, but may choose not to as well. Courses can be offered to build skills, learn more about your industry, learn about the customer service profession, or simply for fun. A great way to offer these is to offer three each month, chosen from the above categories. When choosing a curriculum, do not be concerned with providing classes directly related to the work your reps do. Part of the benefit is simply to allow reps to have fun and build a positive company culture.

I've had great success with classes ranging from wine tasting to Shakespeare. One of my most successful classes was on web design, and was voluntarily taught by a supervisor on Saturdays. The subject really doesn't matter nearly as much as creating an environment where reps are getting something out of it and keeping their minds engaged. It was wonderful to come in on Monday and hear reps talking about what they learned at a voluntary class over the weekend, and it was even better when they took their newly learned web design experience to help create an intranet site for the call center.

This is the type of activity that leads to reduced attrition, since it's these extra opportunities that improve your culture and rep perception of your department and company. Reps will always leave the center for positions at other companies that pay more, as they should, but creating the right culture and learning opportunities through classes and other activities often keeps them from actively looking to leave your company.

Tip 62:
Remove Defensiveness

Before someone can effectively hear and understand any constructive criticism you offer, they must first be in a position to hear it without being defensive.

One of the best ways to do this is to start feedback sessions with a compliment. Recently I attended my son's kindergarten class. After a child reads aloud the next thing that happens is all the other children raise their hands for compliments. As the reader calls on their classmates, he or she is complimented by each person called upon. After many compliments, including some by the teacher, the child is willing to hear any corrections or ideas for improvement from the teacher without being defensive or feeling like they have failed.

In the call center world we provide representatives with constant feedback. To create a positive environment in which reps hear and assimilate the feedback we need to ensure reps receive enough compliments so they can receive constructive criticism without being defensive, as defensiveness often prevents the person from fully accepting the constructive criticism. A good rule of thumb is five positive comments for every negative will remove defensiveness and allow for people to listen to and internalize constructive feedback. If you try this you will find a more receptive audience to your feedback.

Tip 63:
Don't Get "Shouldy"

Here's something I have found useful not only in the call center, but also in coaching my son's baseball team, and in my personal life as well.

For whatever reason, the word "should" instantly feels negative and creates defensiveness on the part of the person you're trying to influence, coach, or train. A far more effective term is to talk to your listener about what they might do differently next time to change the outcome.

Consider the effectiveness of phrasing words in this manner by listening to the following examples and placing yourself in the shoes of the person receiving the feedback.

A. "You shouldn't say, 'Let me finish, I'm trying to help you.'"
B. "Next time, try something like, 'I think I can help, please allow me to explain.'"

A. "You should improve your tone."
B. "Next time try it with a tone that sounds more welcoming."

A. "You should have taken out the trash this morning."
B. "Next time could you take out the trash before going to school?"

A. "You should have swung the bat level."
B. "Next time try using a more level swing."

Feedback delivered with the word "should" replaced with the words "next time" will produce a more receptive attitude toward the information you're giving. And with a more receptive attitude, you see much faster results.

Tip 64:
Lunch for One-on-Ones

Supervisors often feel like they're the busiest people in the company. And truth be told, they may be right. So it's not surprising that I've found supervisors often fail to complete expected one-on-ones for their staff.

Early in my management career, I encountered numerous supervisors who did all their required monthly one-on-ones on the last day of the month, rushing through them to get them completed and often spending as little as five minutes on each one. Obviously these were not effective or productive meetings with their staff. Other supervisors simply confessed to not having enough time to complete the required number of one-on-ones for the month.

Out of frustration I came up with a solution so that no supervisor would ever be able to use the not-enough-time excuse again. Here it is: take your staff to lunch and I will pay for it.

Everyone has to eat lunch. If not, they should at least be *making* the time for lunch. So let supervisors take one of their employees to lunch, have their one-on-one conversation during the meal, and allow them to expense it. For roughly twenty dollars you ensure your supervisors get adequate time with their representatives, you help solidify the relationship between rep and supervisor, and you allow the supervisor to feel like a big shot.

Tip 65:
An Article A Day

Staying up on the latest trends in the call center industry can be challenging. Similarly, educating your supervisors and management team is not something you always have time to do. One way to keep everyone both up to date and focused is to take the "article-a-day" challenge. Just like the name implies, the idea is to read one industry-related article every day. Between industry publications, call center books, and all the information available online, finding an appropriate article is the easy part. The harder part is having the discipline to ensure sure you and your staff commit to it.

My solution is to schedule it on my calendar at 8:30 a.m. Even if I'm not available at that exact moment, having it show up on my computer every day is a constant reminder of this important practice. As far as staff goes, I ensure their compliance by regularly asking them what they read today and what they thought about it. For newer supervisors I often send links and articles to help get them started. Periodically (pun intended) I even have a contest where I offer a small reward to whoever sends me the most interesting article.

A supervisor who follows this will end up reading twenty articles a month, sixty a quarter, and two hundred and fifty a year! So by spending as little as ten minutes reading a day your entire leadership team can educate themselves to a fairly high level in a short amount of time. Articles can keep us thinking about standard best practices and motivate us to follow these practices on a daily basis. And while many articles are written by vendors and don't necessarily have a lot of educational value, the simple practice of reading articles keeps us focused and thinking about call center topics and ways to improve our business.

Another way to implement this idea is to have each member of your team focus on a different discipline within the call center for a month at a time. For example, one supervisor would read an article on workforce management every day for an entire month, while another would focus on call monitoring, and another on motivating reps. In one short month, you'll have three experts who can consult with you on ways to improve your center in their new specialty. After the month is over you might choose to swap them around to create a more well-rounded staff, or you might choose to have them continue to specialize and dig deeper to become real experts in their given areas. Either way you'll greatly expand the knowledge and expertise of your leadership team with very little investment.

Tip 66:
The Full Day Press

A very effective way to improve a rep's performance from me-diocre to good, or, more optimistically, from good to very good is to employ the full day press. The full day press is simply taking an entire eight-hour day to sit with a designated rep.

This concentrated time leads to a number of positive outcomes. You, the rep's supervisor, or whoever sits with the rep, will learn more about the rep in a single day than you otherwise would over a span of weeks, or even months. Think about it—if you sit with an agent and monitor sixty calls in a single day, as opposed to the usual one a week, in one day you'll have heard more calls than you would normally hear in an entire year!

You'll learn about how the rep manipulates their applications and tools, how effective they are at using resources, and a great deal about their work habits. If you sit with a rep in small half- or single-hour increments, the reps will certainly be on their best behavior. But after five or six hours you'll be surprised at how they begin to let their guard down and you can begin to see how they really interact with customers and peers. The time will prove valuable in coming to understand rep's frustrations, since they will inevitably let you know the cause of their troubles – poor training, substandard tools, lack of information—and you'll see and experience many of these things yourself.

If each of your supervisors has a team of ten and you move all their other responsibilities off of them for two weeks, they could spend an entire day coaching, training, assisting, assessing strengths and weaknesses for each of their staff. This can provide a huge boost to a team's performance. I have witnessed this work on a number of occasions. I recall once that for a particularly dysfunctional and underperforming team we cleared the supervisor's calendar for two weeks, and had her devote a full day for each of her ten staff members. After the two weeks was completed the press had completely turned around the team, both in terms of improving skills, and in establishing improved relations with the supervisor. As for the supervisor, she was amazed at the turnaround of her team, and because she now understood the power of side-by-side monitoring, she learned to manage her time to always include it.

Finally, if you're faced with the difficult decision of determining if you need to let a rep go, the full day press will clarify the picture for you, giving you a fairly complete understanding of the agent's performance. Further, from an HR perspective, you will have demonstrated you have done everything you could to attempt to help the rep succeed.

Tip 67:
Self Reviews

A rep self-assessment is a very important part of the review process. Having reps review themselves provides a chance for self-reflection, and also often results in staff empathizing with the supervisor, who is faced with difficult task of rating each employee's performance. During self-reviews staff tend to be honest and even tougher on themselves than the supervisor. This sets the basis for productive conversations on performance and areas for improvement.

Of course, some employees will decide to rate themselves outstanding in every category. In these cases, simply let them know that we all have areas to improve on, and that they need to take a higher standard view of themselves and the department. But for most employees, writing a self-review is a reflective process that helps them come to an accurate assessment of their performance, and be more willing to listen to feedback from their supervisor. Add self-reviews to your review process if they are not already a part of it.

Tip 68:
Giving Reviews

Annual reviews can be a time of anticipation, stress, sometimes frustration, and hopefully for much of your staff a celebration of achievements. Remember receiving a review is always very important to the person getting it, even if the person delivering it may consider it a chore.

Here are some quick tips to improve the delivery of reviews:

If you're delivering a good review, it's good to celebrate the rep's accomplishments over the past year. However, be careful to not overdo it with non-specific praise, which can sometimes set the expectation the employee is about to be promoted, which may or may not be the case. Praise the employee as appropriate, but be specific and realistic in terms how their performance translates into promotional opportunities.

A good practice for favorable reviews is to give the employee a few minutes to read the review and think about it for discussion. I usually bring the person to my office, tell them we're going to discuss the review, and that it's positive overall. I then ask them to read it over while I leave them alone for about five minutes. When I return I ask them if they have any questions and then I review the categories one by one, summarize my comments, and highlight areas of opportunity for improvement. If an employee knows their overall review is positive they'll be more receptive to hearing feedback on areas for improvement. By allowing them to read the whole thing before you discuss it, it removes the concern that there might be some trouble right around the corner.

If you're going to review an employee who has had performance issues and may even be on a performance plan, your HR department will also want to review the documents and ensure everything is worded appropriately. At this point, you do not want any room for misunderstanding.

Make sure the rep hears and understands everything you're trying to tell them. As opposed to the positive review where you might let reps read it by themselves, for poor reviews let reps know you are going to read the review in its entirety and after you have completed reading it, there will be time for discussion. Then read it word for word. Usually at some point while you are reading the review the employee will try to stop you and interject, or argue a certain point of criticism. If they do simply indicate you would like to finish before they comment. Remind them they will have plenty of time to ask questions, seek clarification, and share comments. The goal is to ensure they hear every word that has been written.

At the end of the review ask the rep to sign the form indicating that they have heard the review (for most companies a signature indicates they have received the review, but not necessarily agree with it. Check with your human resources department for your company's policy in this regard). You can then be confident you have followed HR policies to the letter. Again, I highly recommend reading reviews verbatim if you use the review to provide feedback that may be considered negative. This also holds true with warning or other disciplinary memos.

Tip 69:
TGIM (Thank God It's Monday)

Call center agent work is tough, challenging, and does not pay well. Most call center reps are not going to wake up on a Monday and think, "Wow, I get to take calls today! I'm so excited!" But beyond the campaign to just get people to show up, there are many other things you can do to reduce the pain of getting up and coming into the office after a weekend.

For example, start a TGIM program, and do some or all of the following:

Move Friday's benefits to Monday. Many call centers have fun activities on Fridays, such as potluck lunches or dress down days. But Friday has enough going for it by itself. Make Monday casual day and bring in lunch for the crew.

Create a specific Monday-only spiff program. For example, coming in on time is worth a raffle ticket, meeting wrap-up or idle goals are two tickets, good quality scores are worth three tickets, customer compliments worth three tickets. At some point in the day, draw one of the tickets randomly and give away a significant prize. Give other multiple smaller prizes as well. Heap extra praise on reps who have high productivity on Mondays (for most centers this is your busiest day and the day you need it most).

Ensure supervisors spend time walking the floor and encouraging reps. Walk the floor yourself and continually wish everyone a "Happy Monday."

I realize that nothing you can do is going to get reps really excited about Mondays. However, a TGIM campaign can turn Mondays into a more productive day, and you won't have to listen to "I hate Mondays" in the break room.

Tip 70:
Incentive Prizes

Most service centers will occasionally offer contests to promote a certain behavior and build morale, and hopefully you do too (if you don't then start). Common prizes are preferred parking spaces, lunch tickets, goodie bags, and so on, which are all fine prizes. But if you want to provide oomph and really motivate your staff, I recommend you give away cash and TVs.

Cash is always a great incentive. But don't confuse cash with a little something being added to rep's paychecks, where taxes will eat most of it up; and don't confuse cash with a check at the end of the week. Cash is a wad of crisp dollar bills that you carry in your pocket. You walk down the aisles and astonish your reps by pulling out one or more bills and saying, "This is for the high quality score of the day," or "This is for the least amount of idle time today."

You get the idea and your reps will, too. Cash is very tangible and motivating. And at the end of the day, or the beginning of the next day, gathering your reps together and handing out cash is a strong motivator. It's probably the strongest motivator I have ever used. It's not just the money—it's the recognition, it's the tangible reward, it's the instant results. Note, you will want to check with your HR and payroll department to determine to the extent you can use cash as an incentive. To the extent you can use cash, you will find it very powerful. If it is problematic gift cards are an alternative, not quite as dramatic, but can also be very effective.

After cash, my favorite items to give away are TVs. TVs are dramatic, large gifts that really aren't that expensive. Displaying a TV in the center helps build excitement, and it's fun and rewarding to watch the winner lug the TV through the call center on the way to their car. I try to give out a TV and a couple DVD players every year in December.

Another great incentive plan is an auction. Reps earn "center dollars" for meeting daily goals, being caught doing something well, having a great tone, whatever you want to reward. It's fun to create dollars that look similar to a dollar bill but use pictures of department execs instead of presidents. At the end of the contest, prizes are auctioned off during a big center party. You should have enough small prizes so everyone has a chance to spend their dollars, but also a few great prizes for high bidders who have amassed many dollars.

Tip 71:
Non-Monetary Incentives

There are many motivational, non-monetary rewards that can be given out as well. Lunch with a senior executive is a good example. Access and being heard are always great rewards. Also, you could assign a winner of a contest to be on a special project, or assign them a mentor. These prizes are helpful to a reps career and have longer lasting effects than monetary prizes or awards.

One of the most motivating, non-monetary incentives I have ever witnessed in my career was a time we called the parents of star performers. This is something that may not be appropriate in all situations, but when done in the right situation and done correctly has a lasting effect on the employee. In this case I took a couple rising stars in my office individually and told them they had won certain incentives that would be announced later. In addition, I let them know that as a parent I would be interested in my child's successes and asked if it be ok if I called their parents. I got their parents phone numbers and called the parents with the rep present and just said, "Hi my name is Randy Rubingh, your son/daughter works for me and I just wanted you to know they are doing a great job for us. I am a parent and often wonder about my kids, so thought I would call and let you know." The parents we called were extremely appreciative of having been called, and the reps were very thankful as well. Again, I would say this is not the right thing to do in all circumstances, but for reps who are new in their careers, it can have an extremely powerful effect on them.

Tip 72:
Transcribe Wordy Calls

Reps who have wordy calls can be challenging to coach. Sometimes reps talk around a point, repeat themselves, and don't sound articulate or confident. Or they might use a lot of filler words such as "um," "uh," or "like." While theses habits are easy to recognize, and while you can give reps specific and valuable feedback, there are times a rep has trouble internalizing the feedback and using it to improve.

Usually the way to correct this behavior is to have the reps listen to themselves, which provides a great opportunity for them to hear themselves talk and understand what they sound like. Usually after hearing themselves reps will improve immediately.

If you have tried this without success, or you do not have recorded calls at your disposal, another way to drive the point home is transcribe their wordy calls verbatim. It takes some effort to get a call transcribed, but the results will be worth it.

A rep who has talked around the subject, repeated themselves, or used a lot of non-words will very quickly see it on a transcript. A good exercise is to have them cross out all the extraneous words and find their actual answer in the transcript. At this point they're usually left with one or two sentences for every five or six they spoke. Now you can ask them the same question the caller asked them and have them role-play it using the script they have just created for themselves. This is an effective way to help reps improve and maintain their confidence, since they're the ones providing the script.

Tip 73:
Maximize Supervisor Coaching Time

A common frustration for managers and reps is the lack of coaching done by supervisors. Supervisors are often tasked with spending six of their eight daily hours on coaching. But this is rarely achieved, and for a couple legitimate reasons. First, too much of a supervisor's time is spent fighting fires, taking escalations, doing paperwork, and approving exceptions or timecards. To resolve this look for ways to reduce the amount of time supervisors spend doing these functions. Find other resources to accomplish them, or consolidate the functions in a new role. For example, consider creating an escalation desk to which all escalations can be transferred, relieving supervisors of this responsibility. Or if you find approvals take up hours of your supervisors' time every week, hire a supervisor to simply research and make approvals, freeing up those with direct reports to spend more time with their reps.

Another reason supervisors don't spend enough time coaching is the supervisor simply doesn't know how to structure their day to ensure they spend enough time coaching. A best practice is to create a list of coaching activities as a guide. Each supervisor is required to do a fixed number of these activities daily.

For example, the activity list could contain the following:

✓ Conduct a one-on-one meeting with a rep.

✓ Listen to calls with a rep.

✓ Listen to a call side-by-side.

✓ Have a role-play session.

If you require eight coaching activities per supervisor per day, you help the supervisor structure their time, and you ensure supervisors devote maximum attention to staff. If a supervisor has a staff of ten, and each day a supervisor did eight activities from the list above, each rep would receive meaningful attention at least every other day.

Tip 74:
Skip-Level Meetings

As a management level employee moves higher in the customer service organization, inevitably they find they spend less and less time on the floor and begin to lose touch both with the people in the center and with feedback from customers. A good way to stay in touch is through skip-level meetings.

The skip-level meeting is a meeting between a person in the organization and their manager's manager, or even the manager's manger's manager. The skip-level has a number of benefits for both parties:

For the representative it's a chance for them to connect with someone higher in the organization. Not only is this usually considered a perk, but also exposes them to more of the "why we do things the way we do" and the big picture. It helps fill in the blanks.

For the higher-level manager, it helps them keep in touch. The skip-level often lets the higher-up know how well company concepts are being communicated down through the ranks. By skip-leveling they learn about staff they don't often interact with, uncover obstacles they have not heard about, and get a chance to dig into process with someone who has hands-on experience and therefore more familiar with the processes. It's also is great for giving the higher-level manager a chance to assess talent and get to know folks who may apply for positions on their staff in the future.

Tip 75:
Create a "Friend Friendly" Environment

One of the more important factors that results in employees having a high satisfaction with their workplace is the friends they make at work. Given the demographics—predominately young, entry level, friendly and helpful personality types—it's not surprising most calls centers have a lot of informal social activity. Although this occasionally will result in HR issues, generally it is a good thing and should be fostered to the extent you can. You can contribute to the social atmosphere by providing good break room facilities and nice gathering places for employees at lunch or break, such as picnic tables outside and a well-lit and spacious lunchroom. Providing these gathering places will result in more informal interaction, often leading to friendships and strong bonds between employees. This creates a better place to work for them, and lower attrition costs and more satisfied employees for you.

Section IV
Call Center Operations

Call center operations is the management of the day-to-day activities of your service center. Because of the constant shifting of priorities, day-to-day center activity has the potential to create a busyness that consumes the call center manager and prevents you from focusing on the big picture. But this busyness needs to be overcome if you want to move your center from a good to a great one.

The tips in this chapter are centered around themes to put your center on "autopilot," a state where you're no longer constantly putting out daily fires. Once you get to this state you'll not only relieve much stress for you and your senior staff, you'll also be able to take the next steps toward creating a world class organization.

Tip 76:
Soft Openings and Closings

In the morning, as soon as phone lines open, most call centers experience a brief burst of call activity. This spike is caused by customers anxiously waiting for the center to open and calling as soon as it does. Some of these callers attempted to call earlier, heard the closed message with the opening time, and are now calling right at the open. Others may have checked the website for opening times and are also calling as soon as they can.

Typically after this initial rush phone volume will subside, and the second half-hour period of the day is expected to have lower volumes than the first—for some centers, much lower. This creates a staffing dilemma. If you staff for the first half hour you're likely to be overstaffed for the rest of the shift. But if you don't staff for the initial rush, you're likely to be starting the day in a service level hole it may take hours to recover from.

To a large extent this issue can be resolved through a "soft" opening. Having a soft opening simply means scheduling a shift and opening phone lines before the advertised hours of operation. For example, if your closed IVR message, and your website, state you open at 7:00 a.m., staff and open the phone lines at 6:30 a.m. By doing so callers who call early will get through and fewer callers will be calling right at 7:00. If there are no calls, agents can do emails or other work until calls start to arrive.

In addition to smoothing the opening, this strategy provides you early warning if there are system or other technical issues. You have the opportunity to discover and began resolving them before you're technically open. Further, it provides you leeway in case of unexpected transportation or other delays due to weather or other unforeseen circumstances. Be sure to build in the flexibility to quickly change your opening to the actual listed start time in case this occurs. Then when there is a delay in reps getting to work, or minor emergency in your center, "re-close" the center and work to resolve it before your advertised opening. If you're able to resolve the issue quickly, you can open at your advertised time without most customers being affected or even aware you experienced an issue.

At the end of the day centers often have a related problem. First, some callers will be frustrated when they call a minute or two after your closing and suddenly realize they need to call again the next day. In addition, agents who are at the end of their shifts and anxious to leave for home, may rush callers off the phone and not provide as complete of service as you, and your customers, would like. In the worst case scenario, agents will leave with callers in queue who are still waiting for an agent.

To resolve these issues utilize a soft close. Close the phone lines five minutes beyond stated closed times, and have a shift that ends thirty minutes past closing time. Having a shift that ends thirty minutes after the stated closing time prevents reps from being motivated to rush callers off the phone. With thirty minutes left to complete their shift, reps have no motivation to hurry a caller. They also won't dread calls in queue at close that would otherwise force them to stay and work overtime. If the queues are cleared, closers can shift to email or other off-phone work for the remainder of their shift. Or you can send them home as a perk for working what most consider a bad shift, but try not to do this too often since it can lead to the same mentality of trying to rush callers off the phone so the rep can leave.

By keeping lines open for five minutes after close, you eliminate the frustration of callers who call just a minute too late. And by scheduling reps for an extra thirty minutes you ensure callers who call in at the last minute receive the same high quality service as those who called earlier in the day.

Tip 77:
Chat for Internal Support

In many call centers reps who don't know the answer to a customer's question simply raise their hand and wait for a supervisor to come and help. If none is forthcoming the rep leaves their seat and goes to look for someone who might know the answer, or to whom they can transfer the caller.

If you operate this way you're experiencing higher handle time than necessary. If you set up instant chat as an internal support tool for agents, agents can utilize chat to get answers instead of spending time wandering around looking for help. Software for internal chat and chat rooms is readily available and inexpensive, and something most of your reps are familiar with, as they use it frequently in their personal lives.

Despite its benefits, some centers do not use internal chat tools because they fear their agents will spend too much time chatting with colleagues and friends. If this is a concern I recommend creating a work chat room, which has the advantages of providing instant access to help, but lowers potential for abuse.

In the chat room scenario you have an experienced rep, lead, or subject matter expert serving as a chat monitor with agents signed into a single chat room; or depending on your size you may have multiple chat rooms, each serving twenty or thirty reps, and each with an assigned monitor. In addition to providing support, announcements can be made to alert reps to changing situations, latest developments, or to offer encouragement and public praise.

Another benefit to utilizing a chat room, as opposed to one-on-one chat support, is that reps can see each other's questions and the monitor's answers, allowing everyone to simultaneously learn.

If you utilize chat for internal support, keep track of the chats initiated by reps throughout the day. Use these as huddle topics or for additional training. Assume if one rep is asking a question, many others will have the same question. Particularly when new reps hit the floor, there will be a large increase in chat questions. Supply these questions back to the training team so they can see in what areas reps were not quite ready when they hit the floor. In fact, when new agents hit the floor there is usually a short-term need for additional chat agents. Meet this need by having your trainers be the additional help. This provides them direct exposure to topics their students did not thoroughly learn in training.

Tip 78:
Floor Management Schedule

"When everyone is in charge, no one is in charge."

It can be very frustrating to look up and realize despite having a number of supervisors on the floor, you've experienced a run of poor service and no one reacted to it or took measures to improve it. Supervisors and managers often report not having noticed a spike because they were occupied performing legitimate supervisor or managerial duties. Unless you have the size to justify a full time workforce manager to constantly watch the queues, this can be a common occurrence.

A solution to this issue is to create a floor manager schedule. The floor manager schedule designates each management person a shift to watch and be responsible for service levels and make decisions regarding floor coverage and off phone activity. With a floor manager schedule you now have someone accountable for service level at each point in the day. When they're not scheduled as the designated floor manager supervisors can concentrate fully on other activities—one-on-ones, coaching, etc.—confident someone else is watching the floor.

During each shift the floor supervisor should walk the floor with a clipboard containing the current day's schedule, the daily forecast, and all planned off-phone activity. Each half hour the floor manager can log the running total of calls, service level or ASA, emails in queue, oldest email, and/or other pertinent information for your center. In addition, all schedule variances are noted (schedule variances would include reps who call in indicating they will be late, requests to leave early, and changes to lunch or break schedules). If anyone has a schedule variance request they must ask the current floor manager, who, with a glance at the clipboard to see the service levels and other variance requests, can make an informed decision. In addition, the clipboard should also contain a list of possible actions to take if service levels start to slip. For example, if service level drop below sixty percent reassign email agents to phone or request overtime.

As their shift ends, the current floor manager passes the clipboard to the next scheduled floor manager and makes them aware of any pertinent information, such as changes to schedules or off-phone activity. In addition to helping control service level, the floor manager process is great training for supervisors, helping them learn the flow of the center, and creating an environment where all supervisors have a basic workflow understanding.

A quick note about old-fashioned clipboards: Many centers, wanting to go paperless, try to manage off-phone activity without a clipboard and paper, choosing instead to place all information online. If you do this, floor managers may lose the ability to take a quick glance and understand the center's current status while they're walking around. The logging of service level is similar. Yes, you have the same information in reports, but the discipline and practice of actually writing down the information creates an acute awareness of the service levels for the floor managers. This awareness will lead to a better understanding of the ebbs and flows of your center, and better decision making in regards to resource allocation. Therefore, if you implement a floor manager rotation, I highly recommend the traditional clipboard and paper.

Tip 79:
Lower Your Contact Rate

The easiest way to drive down costs and improve your customers' perception of service is to lower the number of times your customers need to contact your service center. Fewer calls translates into less hassle for customers, and with fewer customers needing to be assisted by agents, you'll lower your costs.

As an example of the power of lowering contact rates, I once started a new job and my boss suggested we needed to lower service costs by lowering AHT. I knew lowering our handle time would save a few dollars a month, but at the same time would probably result in reps feeling pressure to rush customers off the phone. I asked him to give me two weeks to sort things out. In those two weeks I determined our contact rate and submitted a proposal for a few process changes that lowered our contact rate from 30% to 20%. This resulted in savings of nearly 25% *and* improved customer satisfaction. In contrast, reducing our AHT would have saved only about three percent and would have potentially lowered customer satisfaction.

To lower your contact rate, you first have to find a way to measure it. Usually it will be contacts (call + emails + chats) divided by the number of orders, or divided by customers. For most companies the proper parameters will be obvious. If it's not for you, think of how you generate revenue. Usually whatever generates revenue—shipments, orders, contracts, customers—will serve as the denominator in the contact rate equation.

For example, if you sell 10,000 widgets per month and you receive 1,000 calls/emails/chats for the month, your contact rate for the month is 10%.

Once you have the contact rate, use your call drivers to find out potential areas to reduce calls. A word of caution, don't necessarily start with the call driver that results in the majority of your calls; start with the one that you have the most control over. For example, if you're getting fifty calls a day that could be eliminated by a quick change in an email confirmation within your span of control, work to eliminate those calls before tackling a call driver that results in 350 calls a day but will take a cross functional team, IT resources, and months of planning to make the product or process change necessary to reduce those calls.

Start with items that will give you quick wins so you can demonstrate the power of lowering the contact rate, and then progress to bigger items. You'll quickly discover that anything that lowers contact rate has an immediate and dramatic ROI. Reducing fifty or seventy-five contacts per day usually relates to a reduction of one FTE, and has immediate payback.

Tip 80:
Creating Actionable Call Drivers

Most call centers are in the practice of logging calls, and yours should too. Reviewing call log reports is a more effective way to gauge why customers are calling you then relying on anecdotal evidence of asking reps, or through spot listening session, or even customer surveys. Call logging is the most comprehensive way to find out why customers are calling you and obtaining direct feedback from them. If you're not currently tracking the reason why customers are calling, you're missing out on a lot of great information that can help you improve the service you deliver.

Use the call log information to reduce the number of calls you receive. This not only reduces expenses but additionally your customers will consider themselves better served if they never have to call you in the first place. In fact, for many service organizations that enjoy the highest service reputations, their reputation is not based on the experience customers have when they interact with the customer service organization, but on the basis of how well the companies execute, and there is rarely a need for customers to interact with them beyond placing an order on the company's website.

The first step in creating call drivers is to pinpoint why exactly customers are calling. Of course there are many CRM systems and many ways to track calls. While a major and expensive CRM system can track the complete lifecycle of a customer and has many advantages, such a system or expense is not necessary to answer the fundamental question of why customers are calling you. So don't let cost or complexity challenges keep you from collecting this crucial information. The information you need to reduce the number of calls can be tallied easily by creating a simple webpage or online tick sheet to track the information.

Whatever system you use, the most important item you're looking to capture is *very specifically* why the customer called you in the first place. This is not quite as obvious as it seems. For example, consider the following sample report:

Report 1	
Called to place an order	25%
Tech support	25%
Order Status	50%

This report is too general. Reviewing this information you cannot determine why exactly the customers chose to call you instead of using your website to place the order themselves, or check their order status online. The information may be interesting, but is not helpful in reducing the number of calls.

What you really want to know is why they chose to pick up the phone instead of ordering from your website. Or you want to know what specific question they asked when they called tech support. Knowing they called for tech support is of little use in reducing the number of calls. In fact, the above report is actually misleading. One might assume simple changes to the order status online have the potential to reduce call volume by fifty percent. This is almost certainly not true. Basic order status inquiries are usually handled online. Chances are these are inquiries as to why something has gone wrong, not for general information. Now consider the following report with further categorization:

Placing Order 25%		
	Coupon wouldn't take	10%
	Customer Received Error message	5%
	Unable to log in	3%
	Cart error	2%
	Wanted to confirm shipping option before placing order	5%
Tech Support 25%		
	How do I upgrade	20%
	Receiving compatibility error message	5%
Order Status 50%		
	Order hasn't arrived (pre scheduled date)	20%
	Order hasn't arrived (post scheduled date)	15%
	No tracking available	5%
	Tracking shows package received, but don't have it	5%
	Package sent to wrong address.	5%

Notice how much more actionable the second report is. Armed with this information you can make a business case for website improvements or other changes to reduce the need for customers to call.

The reason most call drivers are too general is the way they are initially put together. A group often gets together to brainstorm the most common call types and categorizes them. While this seems reasonable, it's rarely specific or accurate enough. A much more precise methodology is to have reps write down the first thing the customer says on the calls they take for a week or so. Then use these exact questions to create your call drivers.

I would further suggest you track "What's the question?" as a free text field in addition to the selected call drivers in your database. This is really the most important information for reps to capture.

When you pull lists of call drivers also pull this field to validate exact reasons customers call you. If you're successful in determining this you can determine the root cause of calls, and drive the rest of the organization to take the necessary corrective action to deflect these calls in the future. And in doing so, you'll simultaneously lower costs and improve customer satisfaction.

Tip 81:
Every Question Once (or EQ1)

Building an effective, internal knowledge database (KB) for your agents to quickly find information will increase their ability to close calls, result in less transfers, decrease the amount of time they spend with customers on hold trying to find information, and allow them to provide more consistent information. To be effective the KB needs to have answers to the questions reps do not know how to handle off the top of their head, and they need to be able to find these answers quickly. Otherwise, agents will either spend excessive amount of time looking for answers, or more commonly just won't use your KB.

Similar to creating call drivers, often creating an initial knowledge database is done by brainstorming common questions and answers. However, again there are problems with this approach. First, it's impossible to think of all the possible questions someone may ask a rep. More importantly, when brainstorming in a room the questions tend to be more general and non-specific, while actual questions from customers are usually specific variances on common questions. As a result the KB has general information but not specific answers to specific questions. To be most effective, you want your KB to list very specific questions and their answers.

Consider for example the common question, "What's my order status?" If this question is in the internal knowledge database, the answer would tell probably tell reps to go to the customer status and read it to the customer. However, in reality customers rarely call and ask this simple question. In cases their question was that easily answered, the customer usually retrieves the information off your website. The real question they ask is, "My package is late—what can you do about it?" or "My order is being shipped to the wrong address, can you re-route it?"

Similar to the previous tip when we discussed the need to log specific questions, it's very important to collect *actual customer questions reps do not already know the answers to* for your internal KB. Once you have them, take these questions and put them in your knowledge database.

The concept of every question once, or EQ1, is to take every question a rep has, research the answer, and then place the question and answer in the KB where it's accessible for next time. If you follow the discipline of EQ1, it doesn't take long before you'll have an extensive and complete KB that addresses all the questions your reps may be asked. If you can do this rigorously over a solid month, you will have answers to almost every question a rep will encounter. To find which questions to use, log all questions from reps to your internal help desk, or have supervisors or leads log all questions they get from reps- these are the ones you want in your internal knowledge database.

Tip 82:
Intranet Site Organization

It's important to create and maintain an intranet site that's effective and useful for your reps. Here you can post bulletin-board type information, provide reps answers to difficult questions (EQ1), and create a reference center for information reps may need to access to assist callers.

However, the creation of useful, practical, intranet site is not as intuitive as it might seem. If you want reps to be able to utilize your intranet while on the phone with callers, there are a couple things to keep in mind when designing the intranet.

First, remember reps using your intranet are looking for answers to tough questions. If the question was easy the rep would know the answer off the top of their head and would not need to look it up. Therefore, do not arrange your information in the logical format of the basic, introductory information and then build upon that in layers of complexity. That's the right way to train, but not the right way to create a useful intranet site. Reps don't want to have to weed through basic information in the search for answers. Consider a school textbook. It starts with basic information and as the student progress the book goes deeper into the subject matter. But too often online information is structured so the rep has to go through the beginning of the book every time they are researching a question. This is a waste of their time.

An effective intranet sites works like reading a textbook from the back, with the glossary up front helping reps quickly navigate to the keyword they are looking for, followed by the harder concepts, the ones they don't already know, and then basic information that people use for training, but will rarely need to access once they are on the phones.

Secondly, make sure the site is intuitive and links are specifically named. For example, if you want to have a link to technical tips, name it for whatever it links to: hardware tips, software bugs, etc. The more specific the better, so "software tips related to 6.0" is better than just "software tips." This will ensure reps don't have to go on wild goose chases while they have callers on the phone, and will save your reps time and energy.

Tip 83:
Flushing the Queue

Almost every call center has a pool of off-phone support person-nel who are trained and able to take calls in a crunch. This pool is made of reps who do support for an offline channel- email or social media for example. The pool can be expanded further by including supervisors, quality analysts, and trainers. When phones spike these resources can be marshaled to help with the phones and control the queues.

Often when it's very busy and the center is overwhelmed, desperate call center managers will assign these off-phone support personnel a shift in order to try to hold the queues down. For example, a center with ten supervisors may assign two at a time to each take a rotating two-hour shift answering phones.

The problem with this approach is you actually only gain two FTEs at a time. With just two additional FTEs you have little ability to affect the queue in a meaningful way, especially considering the nature of high call volume. Poor service levels can be due to a sudden spike, but normally a high queue is the result of call volume building over time as the center gradually falling behind. Often at some point the center is no longer falling behind, yet at the same time isn't able to make any headway against the queue.

For example, consider the case where you have one very heavy hour of call volume. Over the course of this hour the high volume forces the average speed of answer from thirty seconds to five minutes. Volume then returns to normal levels. But the average speed of answer remains at five minutes because while the phone staff can keep up, they're not making headway against the queue. If the queue was suddenly cleared, service levels could be restored and maintained.

So instead of assigning your ten supervisors a two hour shift, have all ten of your supervisors jump in together and completely clear the queue. In this scenario there is a good chance the regularly scheduled reps may now be able to keep up with either zero or one call holding for a substantial period of time. This is even more dramatic in large centers where you may have a pool of twenty or more staff who can take calls, and as soon as they each grab one you suddenly go from twenty calls holding to none. Now instead of every call holding, your center is meeting service level and holding the line. It also takes less time away from supervisors' normal duties than scheduling them each for a couple hours at a time.

In some cases you can automate this clear-the-queue function. If you have an offline group (again, email or social media are good examples), your ACD system probably has the ability to have them work in available and serve in an overflow capacity. If the system has the capability to route calls to them, then you have the ability to flush the queue automatically. For example, if you have ten email agents, create an ACD group for them that activates when ten calls are holding in queue. As soon as ten calls are holding, roll the ten calls holding to this group. If each agent in this overflow group takes just one call, the queue has now dropped from ten to zero.

Now regular call center agents will be cycling back into availability and often can maintain the queue without sustained backup resources. In this scenario there is very little interruption to the email agents' regular work, as they're only assisting with one call each. But for this to work effectively it's important that everyone grab a call as soon as possible. If only one or two agents actually do you will not drop the queue fast enough to allow your regularly scheduled phone agents to catch up.

Tip 84:
Daily Huddles

The call center is often on information overload, continually bombarded with requests and information coming from different sources: new information from product departments, information regarding new marketing campaigns, and internal process changes and updates. While alerting reps to these small changes appears to be a straightforward and simple task, it's actually very difficult to keep everyone informed. Reps are busy on the phone and may not see emails or information you place on your internal intranet site before a customer calls in asking about this new information. You may also face the challenge of having to inform hundreds or even thousands of reps scattered over multiple sites and multiple time zones.

A great way to keep reps informed of all these changes is to schedule a daily huddle or stand up meeting. The daily huddle is a brief, usually ten- to fifteen-minute pre-shift (or as close to pre-shift as possible) meeting to inform reps of changes, or clarify items that seem to be causing reps difficulty. Although resource intensive, the huddle meeting has many advantages over intranet sites and chat rooms for dispensing information—reps can ask questions, obtain clarification, and you can ensure they have heard the information they need.

Try to have your daily huddle between each supervisor and their staff with as many reps as possible at the start of their shift. Here they can share new information, answer questions, and provide a general game plan for the day ahead. The supervisor, of course, must arrive a few minutes early so they can fully assimilate the information before the staff arrives. If not all staff arrives at once, pick a time when representatives are most likely to be available. If there is no new information to share, the supervisor can still make valuable use of the time, talking about statistics from the previous day and publicly praising those who have done a good job in terms of quality, productivity, or other behaviors you want to emphasize. Finally, if you have a daily huddle at the beginning of each shift, tardiness and absences become very public, creating peer pressure for reps to arrive on time and increasing on-time arrivals.

Sometimes you'll need to have an "emergency huddle." This is reserved for those situations you need to inform everyone about something as soon as possible. For some centers this becomes a logistical nightmare. Each team has to wait for the last rep of the team to get off the phone before they can start. With ten or fifteen agents on the phone, inevitably one of them is on a long call, resulting in all the other reps sitting around waiting.

The best way to handle this is to just to grab the closest five or six reps not currently on the phone and share the new information. If you do this efficiently and by looking for people already off the phone, you can minimize the time spent standing around. As reps come off their calls, don't have them join an existing huddle, which will cause you to restart or cause them to miss part of the information; just tell them to go to the next one. Keep repeating this process until you're able to work through the whole center. Eventually everyone will be informed with minimal time wasted by reps standing around waiting for their huddle to start.

Tip 85:
Work-at-Home Options

With advancements in technology it's now possible for most call centers to have agents work from home, processing emails, chats, or even phone calls. Generally speaking, although not always the case, accessing the working-from-home labor pool allows you to recruit a more experienced and better qualified agent. In addition, attrition and turnover from home agents is often lower. However, if your service is complex in nature—that is beyond simple order taking – setting up a successful work at home program where agents are as productive, with as high of quality as internal agents, can be quite challenging.

A basic first step to setting up a program is using a "hub and spoke" model. This is a good way to explore if work at home is right for your organization. Under this model agents are required to come into the office for standard, new hire training. They spend a couple weeks in the center attending training classes and taking calls. Once they demonstrate success they are then allowed to work from their home offices. Many centers that use this approach often have requirements or standards to remain working from home. If an agent is struggling to meet these standards they may be required to come in and temporarily work from the main office, where they can be observed and additional coaching can be offered.

If you're not sure you're ready for a work at home component, or if the only business reason for creating a program is because of space constraints, another option is to create a rotational system. Under this model agents rotate time spent in the office. For example, each might work one week per month in the office and three from their home office. Under this scenario you're able to seat four times as many agents as desks, and at the same time each agent spends enough time in the office to ensure proper coaching and in-house training.

The final option for work at home is creating a complete work from home situation, where reps never actually go to a home office. Recruiting, training, and all work and coaching is done remotely. Before attempting this, use one of the above models as a test to see if your training and support are adequate enough for agents to be successful working remotely.

With any work-from-home model it's essential to connect the agents with the rest of the organization to ensure they're supported and feel like a part of a team. Here are three ways to ensure you keep in touch with agents who work from home. These are things you would want to do for your agents who work in a traditional bricks and mortar call center (they are all tips in this book), but are especially critical for the success of remote agents:

1) Daily short "huddle" conference calls. Be sure to have regular, virtual team meetings. Use this opportunity to keep reps up to date on any information changes, make announcements, encourage, train, answer questions, and receive feedback.

2) Chat to connect remote agents to experts or back line help. With tough questions and complex situations, remote agents do not have the luxury of asking more experienced agents sitting next to them, team leads, or supervisors for advice. Having a chat resource allows them to ask a quick question and receive assistance while talking with customers, preventing transfers and improving service.

3) Provide an intranet site with knowledge databases and bulletin board information. Agents who regularly view the site will keep abreast of the latest information and will be also to quickly find answers to callers' questions.

Work at home is something more call centers will begin to offer as technology continues to evolve and make it more accessible. My advice for those considering work at home options is to start slowly. Test different approaches and carefully track productivity and quality of work for your at home agents. Also, don't conduct all your tests with only your best agents. Allowing your best agents to work from home as a reward for their performance is certainly appropriate. But remember, they are your best agents. Just because they can successfully work from home does not mean your average agents will be able to achieve similar or better results than when they are in the office. Test with agents of all levels before drawing conclusions and forming long-range strategies.

Tip 86:
Schedule Off-Phone Tasks

A t various points in the day you'll see chances to increase effi-
ciency by switching reps to off-phone tasks. For example,
when the phones are slow you might want to shift phone reps to help
catch up the email queue. Or, you may want to seize the opportunity
to have some reps read up on some new information, or have a training session. Some centers just see how it goes, and say they will do
the off-line activity if and when the phones slow down, and will inform reps at that time. But if you use this approach the opportunity
is often lost, or at least minimized due to the amount of time it takes
a rep to get off the phone and start the next activity. I'm sure we
have all experienced having a room full of people waiting for one
rep to get off the phone so an impromptu meeting can start. This is
frustrating for everyone, an unnecessary expense, and a waste of
time.

If you carefully plan out off-phone time and inform every one of the
times in the day when you will be shifting resources, you'll reduce
the amount of time it takes for reps to change tasks and make the
process more efficient. In your morning huddle inform reps of the
times you will be shifting them. Tell them you plan on taking them
off the phones to assist with email at 1:00, or plan on having them do
an on-line training session starting at 2:00. Even if you're not sure if
the switches will be made, inform reps of the possibility. This increases productivity in a couple of ways:

If a rep knows another task is coming up—perhaps one they enjoy –
they're less likely to slow down and coast through their current activity.

They also become mentally prepared for the transition, reducing the
amount of time it takes them to adjust and orient themselves to a

new task. If you just tap someone on the shoulder and ask them to start a training, it will probably take about 10 minutes for them to get started. But if they know in advance, you will save much of this transition time.

Pre-planning also creates a more professional atmosphere. When reps are assigned to switch tasks without pre-warning they often will feel the center is not well run, and they are moved back and forth on whims, which lowers their opinion of management's abilities.

Planning ahead does take some time and organization, as well as a good forecast, but in the long run it means your center will be more efficient and professional.

Tip 87:
Cure the Monday Blues

In this tip I want to talk about the particular problem of sick days being used on busy days—for most call centers this would be Mondays—and a practical strategy you can use to increase attendance when you need it most.

Most centers staff for about a ten percent absenteeism rate, which means if everyone actually came to work on a busy day your staffing level would increase ten percent. But for many centers it seems as though when you most need reps, the 24-hour flu seems to be going around. We all want reps who are actually sick to stay home and get well. But at the same time we need to encourage reps to not call out sick just because they coughed once in the morning, or stayed up too late watching the big game.

To understand the problem, first take a look at this from the agent's perspective. They wake up after the weekend, they're tired, and they know they're in for a day of one call right after the other. They realize they would make the same amount of money if they just called in sick and kept sleeping. The rep makes the call, maybe even simply leaving a voicemail, and a tough day at work has suddenly become a very leisurely day. Don't think it doesn't happen; as I used to say when I was a rep, "Never waste a sick day when you don't feel well."

So is there anything you can do about it? There are policies you can implement around sick days to encourage them not to be used on high volume days and days where they are likely to be used as simply an unplanned vacation day. For example, Mondays might count double in terms of attendance reporting. And there is the rule some centers use of no holiday pay for anyone calling in sick the day before or after a holiday. These policies can be effective, but tend to hurt morale as they imply a distrust of employees.

But simply creating awareness around the tendency to call in sick on busy days can often resolve this issue without the negative cultural effects of creating rules that imply you don't trust staff. To create awareness around the Monday issue simply create a graph that shows the percentage of sick days used by day of the week. In theory, in a call center open five days a week, each day should have twenty percent of the sick days. But in reality Mondays will be closer to thirty percent.

On the Friday before a big Monday, pass this chart out to everyone. This will create the awareness you're watching this and you'll notice if anyone calls in sick. When you use this type of awareness you don't need to be overbearing, or imply someone should come in if actually sick; you simply create awareness and reps will respond and largely self-correct their behavior if it needs to be corrected. I have often passed around this chart before a busy Monday, feigning surprise and curiosity about why this would be so. Every time I have done so, I have seen a dramatic decrease in the number of reps calling in sick the next Monday.

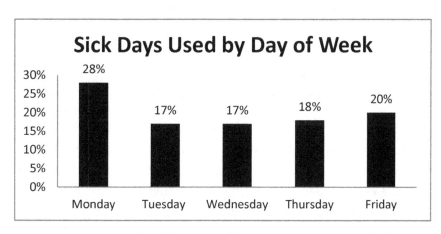

Isn't that interesting?

Tip 88:
Natural Sounding Scripts

Customers often complain, and for good reason, when it sounds like a rep is reading a script to them. When being read a script a customer does not feel like the rep is really listening and understanding the customer's situation. At the same time, reps do not like the idea of reading a script because it often feels awkward and stilted. From a management perspective though, having the rep read a script can seem to be the best course of action because you know the proper information is conveyed in the way you would like it said.

The answer to resolve this dilemma is to create natural sounding scripts. Too often scripts are written with a marketing spin and when they're read they sound great, but when spoken they sound awkward. If you want to create scripts agents will read without sounding scripted, and customers don't feel like they are being read to, transcribe some great calls. Find a call that sounds exactly like you want the information to be conveyed (or role play it until it is perfected). Then transcribe this call *exactly*. Do not correct any grammar mistakes or even filler words. We do not talk in perfect English. A phrase such as "well, it's like this," or "hmmm, I understand, let me ask you this," can make the dialogue sound natural and unscripted. Leave these in your scripts and you will see better rep compliance and customers respond better to the information from your reps.

Be sure your reps understand scripts exist primarily to ensure that specific *information* is delivered to the caller, but that the rep is responsible for adjusting his or her *tone* to mirror the caller. For example, if the caller speaks slowly, the rep should slow down to match the speed of the caller. In contrast, if the caller is a high-powered businessperson who speaks quickly, the rep should adjust their pace upwards and speak very crisply.

Tip 89:
Judge Quality Holistically

A recurring problem faced by many call centers is how to properly judge the quality of individual calls. Most call centers attempt to define all the elements of a call (for example, greeting, offer of assistance, authentication, etc.), put them on a score sheet, and then have a quality monitor or analyst score them as "yes" or "no" for meeting or not meeting that element on the call. When executed well this is a good strategy to measure the quality of service you are providing your customers, and pinpoint areas of concern for additional training. It also gives you a measure of individual rep performance.

However, over time such a methodology leads to what I refer to as a "checklist mentality." Because of fear of being marked down reps become more concerned with ensuring they meet all the check boxes than the customer experience. In one particularly egregious example of this I once heard a rep say, "Thank you for calling Randy, Randy," in order to have repeated the customer's name two times during the call, as that had been defined as the way to make a customer connection. Despite the ridiculousness of this, the quality team scored the call as meeting the requirement. There needs to be a commonsense override that can be deployed by your quality monitoring team to allow for the circumstances of the call, and mark down reps who are obviously not meeting the spirit of the call element, even if they literally do so.

Also consider the example if a caller suddenly says, "I have to go—I have another call." A rep should not be required to try to jam in the normal three or four elements of the expected closing.

Of course, the common sense override is often controversial. But as long as it is calibrated often enough by listening to calls in groups and demonstrating what is acceptable as an exception and what is not, the reps and quality analysts should be able to achieve consistency and agree upon its application.

Another method of doing QA, and the one I prefer, is to do away with checklists altogether. Listen to calls in their entirety and then judge the overall experience of the customer. Were the customer's questions answered completely in a polite and professional manner? What are the areas of improvement in the call? Based on these factors assign the call a letter grade from A to F, just like in school. These grades are generally intuitive and widely understood. Or you could use a number scale such as 1-5, or 1-10.

Again, such methods of judging quality are open to charges by those who will say it's too subjective. But if you calibrate often enough you should be able to get to the point where the grades are consistent and definable, and therefore not subjective at all. And you will find you allow reps to have better conversations with customers, because they can follow the lead of the customer, and are not handcuffed by checklists that dictate what they need to say.

Tip 90:
Internal Quality Scores Trump Customer

M ost managers place the highest premium on satisfaction scores taken from customer surveys, and rank second their internal QA scores. But you should place the highest emphasis on your internal QA scores, while customer responses should be secondary.

Consider that at the point of being surveyed customers have limited information. A rep might have made the customer happy by telling them what they wanted to hear. But if the rep actually gave them false information, the customer, at the point of survey, is probably unaware their service experience is going to be compromised. Conversely, a customer may be upset with something that happened beyond the rep's control. The rep might do a great job from your standpoint, but the customer may take out their frustration with your policies or other factors when they complete your satisfaction survey and mark the rep down. Customer feedback in this way is a barometer of customer perception of your company's overall policies, procedures, and products. But it is not reflective of how well your agent handled the call.

When it comes to judging the service your CS organization is providing, given the limitations reps may be placed under, your internal QA staff has a more complete understanding than your customers. They know the policies and procedures, what the rep can and cannot do, and score accordingly. Therefore, while customer feedback is extremely important for many reasons, especially driving change in your wider organization, it's your internal quality scores that should be considered the most accurate reflection of the service your center is providing.

Tip 91:
Resist Rep Customization

Many systems today allow for individual customization. CRM systems for example, may allow a rep to customize the information on their screen. Their systems may allow individual reps to arrange icons, files, tabs, and other information to their individual preferences. At first glance this seems like a good idea, as some reps may become more efficient by moving data to where it is easily accessible to them. Other reps may just prefer certain color schemes or sizes of layout.

However, usually it's better to not allow customization, at least for new reps. Here's why: during training reps may sit with many different veteran reps, each of who has a different way of doing things. New reps are often told "there are a number of ways to do things – see each one and decide which way works best for you." However, at this stage of their career the new reps do not have enough information or experience to accurately assess the different options. They may find these confusing and are at risk of picking one that isn't optimal. In addition, what if a rep prefers to do something a certain way, but that way results in longer processing times? Is this acceptable to you? Probably not.

So instead of allowing customization, create a standardized approach using the most efficient way with the least amount of confusion. This helps both the new reps who do not need the extra burden of trying to select the best way for them, and controls reps who may prefer a less efficient methodology.

There may be some exceptions to this policy. For example, perhaps some reps are so proficient at multitasking they can handle more windows open on their desktop than the standard employee, resulting in faster productivity for them, while for most reps it would lead to mistakes. You should allow for exceptions for high performing reps who demonstrate productivity or quality gains when allowed to customize their systems. The idea is not to work to the lowest common denominator; the idea is to have everyone start at the same place, a place you know is efficient.

Tip 92:
Email/ Chat Reps Create Own Templates

The exception to the previous tip on not allowing customization is in regard to email and chat templates. Most email/ chat systems have the ability to create templates for universal use. They also have the ability to create hot keys, where a rep only needs to select a few keystrokes to retrieve a template. For example, "shift + s" may invoke the standard template to answer a status question.

However, consistently over the years I have found the best and most productive email/ chat reps disregard the system templates, and create their own templates and templates systems allowing them to quickly cut and paste to create their answers. Continually I have inquired as to why they do this, and have encouraged them to use the standard ones. Part of the reason is good email answers rarely fit a template exactly. The better reps understand this and create phrases and templates to fit their work. They also may find access to the templates cumbersome.

I have learned it's better to facilitate this process than to fight it. In other words, implement tools and processes to allow reps to create their own templates if they choose. Instead of trying to get them to use the standard ones, simply ask them to send all their self-created ones to you on a weekly or monthly basis. Then correct these to the specific wording you would prefer and send them back.

If the standard templates are not complete, perhaps those that the reps are creating should be made available to other representatives. Use the best of these to update your standard templates in the system. Again, from a management perspective it's true it would be better if all agents used the standard ones and simply suggested updates, but experience indicates this will significantly slow your best reps down. If you help them in their efforts, as opposed to trying to get them to conform, you'll find more productive and satisfied representatives.

Tip 93:
Avoid Overflow Double Jeopardy

Most ACD systems have the ability to flow calls from one agent group to another. As a result most call center managers program their systems to queue calls for a certain group of agents, and if those agents are unable to answer the phone within a certain threshold, the calls overflow to a secondary group. However if you do this, be careful to not put your callers in double jeopardy.

Double jeopardy occurs when a caller has to wait for a long time and then overflows to a backup group whose agents are less skilled than the primary agent group. So the customer first endures the wait time, and then is connected with a representative who may not be as proficient or knowledgeable as the agents in the primary group who were intended to take the call.

The way around this is straightforward: Determine quickly if you think the next call will be answered within your threshold; if not, *immediately* overflow them to the secondary group. This way, although the caller may reach a less proficient agent, at least they did not have to also endure a long hold time. Most ACD systems can accomplish this by using an "if" statement at the beginning of the queue. Instead of having your first step of ACD programming be to select agent group A, have your first step be: "If calls in queue are greater than x, select agent group B."

Example 1: Double Jeopardy

1) Route to Agent Group A.

2) Queue for five minutes.

3) Route to less-proficient Agent Group B.

Example 2: Improved Routing

1) If calls in queue or greater than ten, route to Agent Group B.

2) Route to Agent Group A.

3) Queue.

Although the caller may go to a less experienced agent, they do so without any wait.

Tip 94:
Closed Information at Top of IVR

The two most common complaints of customers regarding IVRs are the inability to reach an operator, and going through extensive menu paths only to find the center is closed. Generally both of these complaints are based on the company's desire to encourage customers to self-service.

Tell your callers immediately if you're closed. There's no need to make them go through your menu selection process and waste their time. This is simply going to lead to increased customer frustration, which probably means you'll have an irate caller first thing the next day.

If you simply provide callers the closed message upfront, and still allow them IVR options of self-service if they're available, you'll decrease frustration with your IVR.

Tip 95:
Allow Customers to 0 Out

While call centers are motivated to have callers self-service on the IVR, callers often want the ability to simply zero out and talk to an informed customer service rep immediately. Of course what we know, and customers usually do not understand, is if they don't give us at least a couple of basic pieces of information they're in danger of being routed to an agent who cannot help them and therefore they may need to be transferred. To balance these interests, make it easy to zero out of your IVR menus, but motivate customers to help you at least select the proper agent or group.

To do this, when callers attempt to zero out on the main menu, respond with, "Ok, I'm happy to send you to an agent right away. To make sure we do not have to transfer you, please answer this one question: are you calling about…?"

This approach does a couple of things:

1) You let them know they're on their way to a live agent;

2) You motivate them by "threatening" to transfer them if they don't give you at least some basic information;

3) You let them know that answering a question is helping them, the customer, not just the company.

This has been found to greatly reduce calls to general queues without annoying customers.

This has become even more important as the web has made significant changes in the use of IVR technology and this will continue. In the past, customers received useful information from IVR systems and could often self-service through them. However, now most customers find the information they need on your company's website and only call when they have a question about the information they see on the website. As a result the IVR is losing its importance as a source of information, and is returning to its original function of routing calls to appropriate agent groups.

I believe the next phase of IVR is intelligent routing based on caller profiles and account information. For example, when a customer calls you can now recognize them through ANI (the phone number they are calling from) or other means and quickly dip into their account. Based on account information the IVR should then predict the reason for their call and route them, without asking them to navigate thorough prompts. For example, if the system sees an order in transit and it's past the expected delivery date, instead of having them navigate your routing questions, route the caller directly to a group that can deal with this issue. At this point it's not even valuable to tell them the delivery date, because in most cases they have already consulted the website for this information, and playing it back to them only results in a frustrating delay in getting to a live rep.

Tip 96:
Hosted Solutions

Hosted, or cloud-based solutions, allow a call center to utilize software without purchasing it. Instead, the call center subscribes to the software for a monthly licensing fee and logs into the company's software through the web.

Hosted solutions are becoming more and more prevalent, and for good reasons: they result in low startup costs and provide updates to the latest technology. For an increasing number of companies, especially smaller ones, hosted solutions are increasingly the best option for ACD, IVR, and CRM systems. Hosted solutions also allow for the greatest flexibility in disaster recovery situations.

However, as you increase in size, the subscription model may become more costly than owning equipment outright. Customization may be limited; or worse, customization may be re-set when software is updated. You're also at the mercy of the hosting company's infrastructure—if they go down, you go down. These all need to be considered when weighing the option of an on-premise vs. hosted solution.

Tip 97:
Disasters and Work at Home

With the rise of hosted solutions and VPNs working from home is now a viable option for most call centers, as discussed earlier in the tips under Management.

Even if you do not utilize work from home as a routine part of your service strategy, consider using it at least for a disaster recovery solution- disaster meaning center shut down, weather resulting in staff not being able to come to work, etc. Test in advance if employees can log in from home and access your systems. For most centers, this is true for emails, even if it's not available for phone calls.

Consider providing some of your staff laptops, so in the event of an emergency they can log in from home and process some customer inquiries. Or have a bank of laptops that are tested and ready to go that you can provide to employees if you think there may be a problem with them getting to work.

Even if calls cannot be routed to employees, if they can at least answer emails you can place an IVR message encouraging customers to email you instead of calling. Then in the event of a center closing, you can provide at least some assistance to your customers.

Tip 98:
Plan Emergency Messaging

Almost all sites experience a problem or temporary glitch at one time or another, which leads to an immediate spike in call volume. Unable to access your website customers will call in and queue for a long period of time, only to be eventually answered and told by your reps the reps cannot access account information either. To avoid this scenario you need to be prepared to immediately communicate with customers as soon as an issue occurs. The most common scenario you will want to plan for is to insert an announcement at the top of your IVR or ACD system informing customers you know an issue is occurring, and your reps are also unable to assist at this time.

Messages should be planned for and recorded in advance. Too often companies are hit with a crisis, and by the time they get the message crafted and recorded, it's too late.

To avoid the too-little-too-late possibility, create a bank of all the possible messages you can think of. For example, you can be sure at some point your website will go down, so create a recorded message saying, "We're currently expiring technical difficulties and our systems are down. Please check our website in one hour. Unfortunately our representatives are unable to access account information at this time. We apologize for the inconvenience."

Or, "Please note, at this time our system are down and we're unable to provide any account information; please check back later today. We sincerely apologize for this inconvenience and are doing everything we can to fix this situation as quickly as possible."

Having many different pre-recorded options can make the difference between being able to add a message in minutes, as opposed to hours.

Section V

Outsourcing

Outsourcing, having another company provide customer service on your behalf, has become an increasingly necessary and accepted way of handling a company's customer service contacts. A high percentage of customer service organizations outsource some, if not all, of their customer contacts. The promise of providers of outsourced call center services is they're experts at customer service management, and are therefore able to offer higher quality at a lower price than if you were to build a customer service organization of your own. In reality it's extremely difficult for an outsource service organization to provide a consistent high quality experience to your customers. Outsourcing is a low margin business, and to save expenses providers of outsourced call center services rely on cheap labor. As a result you'll find the reps who staff phones through a provider of outsourced call center services are generally not as well paid or educated as reps employed directly by a company who maintains customer service in-house. In many regions of the country customer service jobs have replaced manufacturing jobs for low skilled workers, and this is true with the labor hired by providers of outsourced call center services.

But this does not necessarily mean outsourcing your customer service will lead to lower quality. What it does mean is that you need to manage and monitor these relationships diligently and continually.

Managing an outsource relationship to provide high service quality to your customers is extremely challenging and requires extensive work on your part. In reality, the provider of outsourced call center services and you (the client) have two different agendas. The provider of outsourced call center services needs to keep costs low while increasing its revenues by adding new business opportunities. You, the client, want to offer the highest possible quality experience to your customers. Your goal is to ensure every customer who calls will remain a loyal repeat customer and will say positive things about your company to friends and colleagues. While the provider does share these goals to a certain extent, their overall objective is to grow their business and keep their costs low.

Outsourcing is most successful when the service is very simple and defined, such as order taking. But if your service is complex, or requires dealing with stressed customers, you'll find outsourcing your business and maintaining a high level of quality to be extremely difficult.

The first four tips of this chapter are directed to the providers of outsourced call center services. Implementing these tips will improve the service the provider can offer to its clients. It will increase the client's satisfaction level, often leading to new business. In that case, it's a win for both sides. The remaining tips are directed to those who outsource all or a portion of their customer service. The tips will help you manage the outsourcer relationship and drive the outsource provider to improving the service they provide your customers.

Tip 99:
Transparency Increases Credibility

Quite possibly the number one thing that breaks down credibility between a service provider and their client is the provider's claim that "everything is going great." An involved client will not accept this statement at face value. The involved client will monitor calls for at least an hour a week, look at productivity reports every day, and know the reps from site visits and conversations with them about how they like their jobs and working for the outsourcer.

With access to this much information inevitably the involved client will know and understand the issues in the center. So when the provider tells the client that "everything is great", the client can only conclude the provider either does not know or is not willing to admit the issues in their center. Either destroys confidence in the provider and its leadership team.

On the other hand, as the representative of an outsourcer, if you simply acknowledge issues, the client usually will assume you have a handle on them and you can be trusted to address and correct the issues. This truthfulness establishes a valuable framework of honesty and respect. But when issues are not acknowledged, I, as a client, conclude I must be even more engaged in the management and oversight of the service provider's call center.

Tip 100:
Be Proactive

If you're a provider of outsourced services and want to create a lasting partnership with your clients, take a proactive approach to their account. Come up with new ideas, drive improvements, create reports, and make suggestions on process or product improvements.

With rare exceptions, clients never feel they're given too much information by their provider, I never have. In fact, the more information the provider pushes to them, the more they assume the outsource management is watching over their service and taking care of their customers. The more a client hears from their outsource partner, the more they tend to leave them alone. This is good for both the client and provider. The provider doesn't want their business constantly disrupted by the client asking for information, changing processes, or coming up with ideas that may not be practical. And the client doesn't really want to be involved in the day-to-day management of the center; if they did they would not outsource it in the first place.

The way for a provider to avoid the client being overinvolved is to be proactive. Take the initiative. Be the one to talk about what's going on in the center and how it can be improved. Tell the client about incentive plans you're running for reps and what's being discussed on the floor. Give them both the good and the bad, ask for more calibration sessions to ensure quality is viewed the same by you as them. The more information provided, the less tempted the client is to either try to run the service for the provider or find another solution.

Tip 101:
Know Your Service Organization

Know more about your service organization than the client does. This may sound easy; and with clients who simply write checks to you every month without any real involvement, it is. But clients who are engaged and actively manage their account will know who the good reps on the account are, have a feel for the level of morale, and intimately understand the service levels and how well the management team reacts to them. It's important the executive management team of the provider knows and understands the issues at a more in-depth level than their involved client.

The problem is account executives for the provider may know the overall service levels, but don't always know the reps and detailed problems of various accounts. The supervisor knows the reps and issues on the floor, but doesn't necessarily see the whole picture. So too often the only person who has a complete overall perspective of the service provided by the outsourcer is the client. This leads to a lack of confidence in the provider and is why, as a client, I may begin taking calls from the sales rep of other providers.

As an outsourced service provider, ensure there are people in your organization who have a complete account perspective and have those people be the main point of contact with the engaged client.

Tip 102:
Make a Recommendation Every Six Months

During implementation of a new outsourcing relationship the outsourcer often claims the client can expect regular recommendations on how to improve their business. Most clients would be receptive to and even love to hear these recommendations and incorporate them into their business.

Sadly, despite the promises and best of intentions, experience indicates providers rarely make even one practical recommendation that could be implemented on how to improve the service of their client companies. Perhaps this is because once the initial consultant/selling phase of the relationship is over, the business is turned over to an operational team who is generally challenged with just keeping the business running and attempting to meet service levels. These people may not have the time or the experience to step back and look at the big picture. Or perhaps they feel making suggestions will lead the client to conclude things are not going well. Whatever the case, staying silent is the wrong approach.

The key for you as the provider in making suggestions is not to over-reach. Just attempt to make one significant, realistic, easy to implement recommendation to your client every six months. For example, look for an opportunity to automate some calls or emails, improve a process, or increase the knowledge levels among your staff with some support from the client. Try to make recommendations you know are within your contact's sphere of control, as opposed to strategic direction or recommendations requiring extensive system resources, that while may be valid, are often impractical as they're difficult to implement. By simply making one or two quality, practical recommendations a year you'll become a trusted and valued partner.

Examples of quality recommendations:

1) How to automate calls, maybe through IVR or simple website changed.

2) Proactive emails that could be sent to reduce the number of calls.

3) Areas the staff need training help (but please don't pass this all over to the client). Offer to interview the client's subject matter experts on the topic for an hour and create training out of it.

4) Ideas on how to obtain information needed in the center on a more continual basis. If the center is always hearing about changes from customers, discuss these with the client, and find out where and when these become official and how you might be involved earlier in the release process. Offer to participate in some of the client's internal meetings so your contact will not have the burden of relaying the information to you.

5) Create training materials and send them over to the client for correction and approval.

6) Collect and share data on the types of calls received.

7) Share the pain points of customers. Provide reports showing in what areas and under what circumstances customers are frustrated with the company and become irate.

Even if your client is unwilling or unable to implement your recommendations, simply sharing the information will keep your clients satisfied and give them confidence in your ability to manage their service.

Tip 103:
The Five Cs of Outsourcing

(Editor's note: This tip is based on a recent seminar presentation I gave on outsourcing. As a result, much of the information is also included in other parts of this section; please excuse any redundancy)

Here's a tip aimed at both clients and providers. Outsourcing has become an increasingly accepted way of managing customer contacts. But as we've mentioned earlier, the provider and the client have two different agendas. The provider needs to keep costs low while increasing its revenues by adding new business opportunities. The client wants to offer higher quality at a lower cost.

Outsourcing is a low margin business, and often involves hiring cheap labor. As a result you'll find the reps who staff the phones are not always effective at providing exceptional service. I understand all providers will deny this, but I base this on my twenty-five years in the call center business and having managed numerous outsourcing relationships.

But all of this does not necessarily mean that all call center outsourcing must result in lower quality. What it does mean is that you need to manage and monitor these relationships continually and consistently.

The key to a successful outsourced relationship is following what I call the Five Cs:

1. Communicate

An account manager's main goal for an outsource company is to increase its revenues. The best way to increase revenues is to please the customer so they outsource more of their business to the provider. This makes good sense. Unfortunately, this also means that it's in the provider's interest to communicate to the client only the account's highlights and accomplishments. From a provider's perspective, the less the client has to think about service, the more successful they will consider the relationship.

Clients meanwhile, especially those who are not close to their customers, have a tendency to think their products and services are perfect. As a result, they're all too willing to take the provider's word that everything is great. When this happens we find the client and provider both communicate on a superficial level, the reps at the provider are not well informed, and the client doesn't get crucial feedback from its customers. At this point service deteriorates.

Communication between the client and provider has to be honest. For the client it's essential to tell the provider all the product related problems and issues you're aware of, so they can deal with them in service. Too often the client is concerned about confidentiality and doesn't provide the full picture, but this strategy is doomed to backfire since outsourced reps won't be prepared for customer calls.

In the same way the provider needs to be completely honest with the client. If the client is eventually surprised by negative feedback from customers, or from customer surveys, they will be disappointed the provider didn't provide this information earlier, and may begin to doubt the effectiveness of the provider. Both sides of the outsourcer equation must agree to be completely honest in order to make the relationship work.

The best way to accomplish this is to make communication continual with honest, weekly meetings where both sides have a chance to talk openly about current performance, and what is happening within both organizations.

2. Collaborate

Ensure the client and outsource management teams view the quality of emails and phone calls the same way. Have quality teams from both the service provider and the client score calls and emails together so there is common agreement on scoring. The QA scores provided by either the provider or the client should be a realistic assessment of the current state of service being provided. Many times calibration sessions are done only quarterly or monthly. But if you really want to achieve a high level of service for your customers this is not frequent enough. Calibrate at least weekly, and when you begin an outsourcing relationship, do it even more often.

3. Commiserate

Openly share and discuss each other's problems. The client should take a realistic view of the difficult situations they often put the outsource reps through—poor performance of internal systems, or products and service not rolled out well. These situations will result in service degradation that is the result of actions, or lack of action, by the client. The client should own up to these and provide allowances when their service provider struggles under these circumstances.

In the same way, the provider needs to acknowledge where they have come up short. As an experienced client I can empathize when a provider is put in a difficult situation, and if they're honest about it I will work to help them.

But if they paint a rosy picture, I expect great results. Hiring is a typical example of this. It has often been the case I have asked a provider if they can hire a large number of agents in a short time period. Those times they have assured me it would be no problem and then came up short, I have been very disappointed and made my disappointment clear. But for those times they laid out a hiring plan and showed me their efforts and the risks based on the time frames I asked, I have worked with them and understood if they came up a little short. The key is honesty and expectation setting.

4. Commit

Providing quality customer service for a company other than one's own is extremely challenging. Both parties must commit to making the time and financial investments to make it work. The client needs to dedicate resources to ensuring the provider has all the information and support they need. The provider needs to commit to a continual improvement process and to keep working to improve, even when the client makes it difficult.

5. Castrate

If we don't get it right we chop them off. Okay, if you want to be nicer you could substitute "compensate" for "castrate," but castrate really makes the point. There should be momentary rewards and penalties to back up commitments. Risks and rewards should be established to promote an environment where both parties benefit from efforts that result in higher productivity and higher quality. Likewise, there should be fees at risk and penalties to motivate improvement if agreed upon KPIs (key performance indicators) are not met.

Tip 104:
The Contract/ SOW

Negotiating a statement of work (SOW) with your provider can be a grueling task. But it is also very important and something where time needs to be invested to get it right. Here you will spell out the responsibilities of each party in the relationship and, very importantly, lay out terms and conditions for financial risk and rewards.

A couple of notes about SOWs: when creating risk / reward fee structures the goals for financial incentives should be at the level to save you money. For example, if you have a risk/ reward for handle time, make it so that if you are paying out a reward the amount of the reward is less than you would have had to pay to hire additional reps if the goal had not been reached. A reward of a dollar more per hour for billable hours can add a lot to your monthly bill. But if the productivity reached means you can reduce your staff by 10%, it's worth it, if you reduce your staff by only 3%, it may not be worth it. Be sure to do the math when setting the goals.

It's also important to understand how risk/ rewards translate down to the rep level. If you find yourself in the situation where you see reps are being put in a squeeze between their goals—created to meet the SOW goals from the outsourcer standpoint—and the needs of your customers, quickly renegotiate the SOW. This most commonly happens in regard to productivity scores. You set up a productivity risk/ reward with your outsourced service provider, the provider in turn creates individual handle time goals for the agents. In theory these are not your concern. But if you spend enough time with the agents you may learn they feel pressured to wrap up calls very quickly and hurry callers off the phone, even though they believe it's causing them to provide a lower level of service than they desire and feel is right. Here you have a conflict where the productivity risk/ reward is not translating well to the floor and needs to be reevaluated, or at least balanced with corresponding quality goals.

Same is true of closure rates. Let's say you have a risk/ reward for first time closure rate. In turn the outsourcer creates a rep incentive for cases closed on first contact. This makes sense. More cases closed on initial calls will save you money from decreased call backs. However, you need to balance this with a penalty for cases reopened. If you don't, and reps feel pressure from their management team to close as many cases as possible, reps will quickly learn they need to do everything they can to close a case, and may close ones that really should remain open.

Tip 105:
Visit Until They Stop Taking You to Dinner

A major challenge when you outsource customer service is losing contact with your customers, as well as losing contact with the front line agents who serve your customers and have valuable information about your products and services. Make up for this gap through site visits on a regular and consistent basis. Nothing can give you a clearer picture of the situation faced by service representatives, and the type of service being provided, than to actually be onsite.

In terms of how often one should visit their outsourced service provider, I think a great rule of thumb is to visit the site often enough so the managers and staff no longer feel as if they need to continually be polite to you. If you're there only rarely, your visits will be a rehearsed show. Everyone will tell you how wonderful everything is and they'll wine and dine you. However, once they're comfortable with your frequent presence they'll begin to drop their guard and let you know how things are really going. They'll even stop taking you out to dinner! This is a good indication you're visiting enough. At this point the reps will often trust and confide in you, giving you valuable information on the culture and how the reps and your customers are being treated. You'll learn so much more and your visits will be much more effective than when you are in well-rehearsed meetings and dinners with senior executives.

Tip 106:
Sit on the Floor

Too often when a client visits the provider the client sits in a conference room doing email, interrupted by an occasional meeting with the outsourcer's senior management staff. This is a missed opportunity. When you visit an outsourcer spend as much time on the floor as possible. Spend time sitting with reps and listening to them as they take calls. At first this may be awkward, as reps may be intimidated by a visiting client executive. However, if you are friendly and disarming the reps will eventually come to see you as a powerful ally and will began to open up to you. This gives you the inside scoop about what life is like in the center, and what it's like for your customers. Insights learned on the floor will provide valuable feedback about what's going on in the center and what improvements need to be made. Make good use of your frequent visits to your outsourced service center by sitting with reps and learning about what their jobs are really like.

Tip 107:
Make Your Success Their Success

One of the difficulties in outsourcing is that the success of an outsourced program, as well as the success of individual employees is not always directly connected to *your* success. For example, at an account level, increased call volume leads to *increased* revenue for the service provider, while your costs rise and overall satisfaction of customers will *decrease* due to their need to place a call.

On the individual level, if a rep or supervisor is successful on your account they may be able to create more opportunities for their own career growth. But in order to take advantage of these opportunities they may need to switch to another account, resulting in you losing a rising star. As you can see at some point your interests and those of your service partner diverge. So, at both an individual level and a corporate level, it's important to do everything you can to tie your success together.

On the individual level, be sure to work with your provider to provide incentives to employees and opportunities for them to grow. If management opportunities on your account are limited, consider creating positions at the provider that you might have in-house—process improvement experts, for example. Also, work with the provider on individual rep and management bonus programs; even fund them if necessary, as this may be an important retention motivator.

On the corporate level, this can usually be done with incentives that motivate the upper management team to provide recommendations and innovations to improve the business and customer experience. Often these are difficult to actually quantify, but to the extent you can, it's certainly worth it. For example, if you're currently paying

$4 per call and the outsourcer provides a solution to reduce call volume by 1,000 calls a month and it works, bonus them $2,000 a month for the next six months for the calls they helped eliminate. For them this is now pure profit without any operational issues. Or, create an executive bonus program where you pay the upper management team members discretionary bonuses based on practical recommendations to improve the business. If a manager gives you a recommendation that will save you $50,000 annually going forward and you give him a bonus of $10,000, this motivates him to continue to make recommendations, and you're making significant cost reductions.

Tip 108:
Be Their Best Account

U sually at an outsourced center there are multiple accounts, and the pay and culture will be slightly different depending on the particular account a rep works for. Reps, and management personnel, often have opportunities to move from one account to another, either as a promotion or lateral move. They make this decision based on a combination of the reputation of the cultural differences of the accounts, pay rates, and promotional opportunities.

You always want to position yourself as having the "best" account at the outsourcer—the one that attracts transfers either because it's the best paying, the most fun, or has the best perks. Having high internal interest is a key to success, as it lets your account team pick from the best internal candidates. Being internal these candidates have a known track record, so if you can generate a high level of interest in working on your account you can pick from the best of the best. Work with the outsourcer to find out how to become the best account to work for, utilizing pay, culture, company perks, or empowerment. I mention empowerment because although it can be complex to determine appropriate authority levels, particularly with an outsourcer, lack of empowerment is a driver of employee dissatisfaction.

Tip 109:
Rep Quality Vs. Exec Quality

When deciding to outsource you'll inevitably face a choice of using a large provider with many sites and thousands of agents employed, or choosing a smaller "boutique" provider which may only service a handful of clients with a few hundred agents. As a general rule you'll find large providers generally have better management teams, but smaller providers generally have better reps.

The reason for this is simple: As an executive you have many more career opportunities at a large provider and will naturally gravitate there. Providers that spend their money on executive talent have less to spend on agent salaries. They attempt to make up for this by providing "systems" and programs to prop up less experienced or educated reps. The extent to which this works is usually dependent on how much the local management buys into the programs and their willingness to implement them.

On the other hand, small providers generally don't attract the same caliber of executive talent and are more likely to promote from within to fill their management ranks. As a result, top management recruits may not look to these companies because they may have limited opportunities; but on the other hand, they generally pay their reps better, attracting better agent quality. And because management may have been promoted from within, they are closer to the floor and have a deeper understanding of rep issues and how things really work.

So which one should you choose? That depends on the type of service you're considering outsourcing. On the one hand, since rep turnover is high, so you may want to choose an experienced management staff that will undoubtedly be more stable. On the other hand, it's really the reps who make the difference. I think the answer lies in how mature your service environment is. For centers that are highly structured and whose processes and procedures are stable and well documented, a large provider's ability to scale is often the better choice. For fast-changing companies that require a deep agent understanding, smaller providers are often the better choice, at least ones with very high and obvious agent quality.

Tip 110:
Provide a Dedicated Resource

While it's obvious, it's important to continually keep in mind your outsourcer service provider only knows what you tell them. They do not benefit from "company osmosis"—the frequent meetings, emails you're copied on, and casual hallway conversations that keep you up to date on your company and help you make service decisions.

Without the benefit of this casually circulating information, the service provider may not be able to connect all the pieces to resolve certain service issues. At times due to lack of information reps may be forced to make an educated guess. Educated guesses seem like a good idea, and sometimes are, but there are times this will result in customers receiving incorrect information.

This is not so much the fault of the rep, but the fault of the company that didn't share all necessary information with their service partner. Usually this is not intentional. Clients don't make it a practice to withhold information from their provider. Rather it's the result of the client assuming and planning on best-case scenarios, and not considering all the possible complications and questions to new products and services.

To overcome this challenge there needs to be constant two-way communications. First, the client needs to communicate all changes, no matter how small, and share all outgoing customer communications, so the outsource reps don't hear about these changes from customers before hearing about them from the company.

Second, the provider needs a channel to ask questions when they are not sure of how to respond to a customer inquiry. These should be funneled through a dedicated resource at the company who serves as a liaison between the outsourced service partner and the client company. Ensuring a client resource is available at all times will eliminate much of the need to "guess", or make assumptions on the part of the outsource provider, ultimately resulting in better service to your customers.

Wrap Up

The call center business is a fairly new industry, but at the same time is a rapidly changing one, as it has been since its existence. With the pace of technology in our industry, the rise of importance of mobile communications and social networking, one can be sure many changes are to come over the next few years that will completely change the way we service customers. It's entirely possible that within the next couple years, much of what I have written will need to be updated.

Nevertheless, many principles remain the same as when I started in this business twenty-five years ago. Customers still want to be able to get through the clutter and interact with an intelligent person who can help them resolve their issue as soon as possible. Agents want to be treated with respect and have career opportunities. While contact methods may change I don't think the core of human interaction changes. I have heard it said many times in my career, "It's only business." That may be true, but our business is people.

There is a science behind running an effective call center. I hope you have learned some of that science through reading this book and you are able to successfully implement some of these tips. If you do, I'm confident you will "launch" your organization to great heights of employee and customer satisfaction. **Good luck!**

Randy Rubingh

R andy has more than 25 years' experience building, managing, and leading customer support organizations. He has led service organizations ranging from small start-ups with as few as five agents to leading a five-site, international customer service organization with thousands of agents. During the course of his career he has managed over 20 million incoming phone calls. His service strategies and opinions have been profiled in numerous industry publications, and he is a frequent conference speaker. Randy lives with his wife and two sons in the San Francisco Bay area.

Made in the
USA
Monee, IL